Behind the Scenes at Radio Caroline (in the 1970s)

Lyn Gilbert

ACIP catalogue record for this book is available from the
British Library

ISBN 978-1-9999334-8-7

Published by Woolloomooloo

Typeset by Designed Memories

Cover photograph copyright Foundation for Media
Communication Rob Olthof

This book is dedicated to all those, past and present, who were involved in keeping Radio Caroline on the air.

Introduction

There have been a number of books written by people who were involved in Radio Caroline in the 1960s – which included Caroline North and South. Other published books have covered the 70s, 80s 90s and more recent years. Each has had a unique story to tell – either from their perspective and personal involvement or through research, interviews and information gathering. None tell the whole story. That would be impossible. From its inception in 1964 up until 1967, the organisation was huge with many people involved. After the Marine Broadcasting Offences Act (MOA) came into law in August 1967, Caroline had to operate clandestinely. Ronan O'Rahilly – Caroline's main initial founder decided he would continue with Caroline when many competing stations (such as Radio London) closed down. He began to restrict details of what each individual who worked in the organisation knew. He would weave plausible stories to those he encouraged to work for Radio Caroline for very little financial reward, and compartmentalise the different projects he was running. It was the only way the projects could continue to exist.

Although I was involved in various projects of Ronan's from 1974 - 1980, I didn't know the full details of how everything worked. I didn't want to know and asked few questions; only those pertinent to my work. Perhaps, because I didn't ask too many questions, Ronan was forthcoming with a plethora of information – although I realised over time, he told me only what he wished me to know and I suspect not all of it was true.

With the passing of years, some dates have become blurred and I cannot always pin down the precise chronology of events. I did not keep a diary. I have prompts from my old passport, letters, memory and other memorabilia. I might have forgotten specific dates, but not the events.

My story and involvement with Caroline was interwoven with the documentary film Ronan was funding about the assassinations of John and Bobby Kennedy and Martin Luther King. I cannot talk about my part in Radio Caroline without including it.

Some names have been altered to protect identities. Where I use real names, it's either because they have already been used in previous books published about Caroline, are well known in the music industry or are no longer alive. With crew and presenters, I have used their 'professional' names. Their real names may have been plastered over various websites, but I'm sticking to the ones we used on Radio Caroline.

1

Under the cloak of darkness, the Mi Amigo was waiting to be towed out to sea. Presenters and other crew had been waiting below deck for some time. Some had been on the boat for weeks. Others had sneaked on at the last minute.

The tugboat captain was waiting for the all clear; suspicious as to why they were leaving at such an ungodly hour. Clearance papers had been passed to him with the story that they wanted to anchor in position and give the crew a full working day to set things up.

The man standing near the docks watching events knew the tugboat captain was radioing to someone. He'd asked many questions and he now suspected the captain was attempting to get hold of someone from the Scheepvaartinspectie to verify the clearance. The papers were in order so he knew that wouldn't be a problem.

3

What might be a problem is if he found out Ronan still owed money to the company which had carried out the repairs. Ronan had assured him that the bills would be paid – eventually. They needed to get the ship fully fitted out and back on the air to generate some income first.

He'd asked Ronan whether they were going to be broadcasting as Radio Caroline as he knew Ronan had been in discussions with various potential backers from other radio stations.

'Not immediately. But soon,' Ronan had replied, refraining, as usual, from imparting much information.

At last the tugboat started to move. He watched for some time until he was sure they weren't going to be intercepted before setting off to find a phone box.

Some miles away the phone rang waking Ronan from a deep sleep. He'd had a late night, discussing options with potential investors and waiting up to hear the news, but sleep had eventually found him.

'It's me. They've gone.'

'Great to hear. I'll see you soon,' he said hanging up. Talking on the phone had to be done in short sentences and code – just in case anyone was listening. The Marine Offences Act of 1967 had meant that broadcasting Radio Caroline was illegal, unless it was outside territorial waters. Once the Home Office heard that Caroline was up and running again, he was sure they'd be tapping his phone and the phones of all those associated with him. They might have already done so, if the Dutch authorities had passed on information about the test broadcasts they'd carried out recently.

He could just picture the look on their faces once they learned Caroline was back.

2

Chapter one covers the 'story' Ronan told me in 1973 about 'hijacking' the *Mi Amigo* and sneaking it out of the docks in Amsterdam and Ijmuiden in 1972. He exaggerated it considerably from the scaled down version I've written. As I sat listening to him, I imagined scenes from an episode of *Danger Man* I'd seen where men in dark clothes climb aboard a ship at night and take control of it. He justified the actions he'd set in motion explaining that the ship had been *stolen* from him some years before and he needed to rescue it before it was sold for scrap. He only mentioned the one boat and not being a resident of England during the 1960s, I had no idea that there had been two boats broadcasting; Caroline North and Caroline South. I was later to find out that the second, larger boat, had already been scrapped.

Ronan told me he bought back the Mi Amigo ship but couldn't afford to pay for all the repairs that were necessary. He did pay for the ship but failed to mention that he 'borrowed' the money from a man named Norman Lambert whom he never paid back.

I first met Ronan in 1973 at a party being held by his friend, Oonagh at her home in West Hampstead. At the time I was renting a 'flat' from Oonagh that consisted of a large bedsit, plus kitchen/diner and shower room/toilet, on the ground floor of her house. The majority of her living accommodation was on the basement/garden level – although she retained a bedroom between my front bedsit and my kitchen/diner for her son Tadgh. I had been living at the West Hampstead house since the late summer of 1972 when Oonagh offered me the 'flat'. I'd spent months attempting to find somewhere to live while staying with a group of Aussie journalists in WC2. I wasn't supposed to be in the WC2 house as I had a young baby and most tenancy agreements precluded occupation by young children. As soon as I mentioned to potential landlords that I had a young son, they shook their heads and said 'no children'. Oonagh proved to be the exception and I will be forever grateful to her for being willing to rent to me. She said she had been in a similar position once with her son Tadhg (pronounced tige). We quickly became close friends.

Oonagh was short like me and I learned that she had the majority of her clothes made to fit. Knowing I would have the same trouble she put me onto Bonny, her dressmaker, and thereafter, for many years, Bonny began to make my clothes. Up until then I'd had to take up any trousers or long dresses (which were the fashion then) I bought. Including the one I was wearing at the party where I met Ronan.

I couldn't say whether the party was held in the

winter, spring or early summer of 1973. I know I was wearing a white Indian Cotton style dress with red embroidery. However, during colder months Oonagh kept the Central heating blasting out so that she could wear her summer dresses all year round.

Central Heating was something I hadn't encountered before coming to the UK. Born and raised in Australia, most of our homes were heated by coal/wood open fireplaces in the living room only. When gas fires became more readily available, they replaced the open fires. Other rooms in the house weren't heated – even if they needed it in the winter. The house in WC2 had central heating but it was kept on a low temperature and I survived it without difficulty.

At Oonagh's house, I struggled with the intense heat. I turned all my radiators off and opened the windows but the rooms were still really hot from the pipes running under the floor. I was also working in an office that had the heating blasting out all day with no fresh air. As a result, during the colder months, I developed continual bouts of conjunctivitis and spent a lot of time at Moorfields Eye Hospital.

My eyes were clear on the day of the party and Ronan plonked himself down beside me on the couch and said 'You're Irish, aren't you?' I had long chestnut brown hair.

'No, I'm Australian,' I told him, exaggerating my Australian accent. He hadn't introduced himself.

'Ah. You must have Irish ancestry then,' he continued.

'Some,' I said nodding, reticent to elaborate. My

maternal grandparents were Irish and there were Irish great, great grandparents on my father's side.

He introduced himself then and I realised he was the man Oonagh had worked with in the 1960s. She'd told me various stories about their working lives. After telling him my name he leant over and asked me what I had been doing the night John F Kennedy had been shot.

I frowned at him. Why did he want to know this?

'Do you remember his assassination?' he asked.

'Of course I do,' I said without elaborating.

'Are you going to tell me where you were and what you were doing when you heard about it then?'

I sighed. I couldn't see why this man would find my account interesting but I launched into. 'Okay. I was in my bedroom, supposed to be asleep but I had been listening to the radio and reading until the small hours of the morning. I'd just turned off the light when I realised I hadn't done my Geography homework, so put the light and radio back on and started on it. A news flash came over the air saying the president had been shot. I was shocked and waited for further news. A later bulletin said he'd died. I cried my eyes out and didn't get any sleep at all. John F Kennedy was my hero. When he was first elected president, I used to keep a scrapbook on him and his family. I was only a kid.'

I felt a bit embarrassed to be confessing my hero worship of a man who had nothing to do with my country.

Ronan broke into a huge grin, leaned across and said,

9

'I think I'm in love with you.'

I laughed at him, and jumping up, went off to refill my drink.

I can't recall at what point in the party the firemen arrived. Apparently, Ronan had had some difficulty finding Oonagh's particular street so had called into the fire station to ask for directions. He invited them to the party. A large fire truck pulled up in the dead-end street and several enormous firemen came into the flat. One of the other men at the party was overjoyed. He had always wanted to sit in a fire truck so the firemen took him and Oonagh's son Tadhg out for a spin.

Ronan was pleased that he'd brought someone so much joy and sat grinning from ear to ear.

Later I was sitting on the couch again eating a curry that Oonagh had cooked and he joined me with his own plate of food. At the time I believed it to be an accident, but later when I thought about it, I decided his actions were deliberate. Ronan's left hand knocked the plate of food I was holding, spilling it all over my white dress. He was very apologetic and someone, possibly Oonagh, rushed over to help me clear up the mess. My dress was covered in curry stains though so I left the party, went upstairs to change and put my dress in a bowl to soak in the kitchen (contrary to my expectations all the curry stains came out and the dress was like new again).

Not long afterwards Ronan burst into my kitchen, claiming he'd come to apologise again. Oonagh had told him where he might find me. I wondered later if he'd thought he might catch me in a state of undress.

I made a pot of tea and we sat in that kitchen for some time, with him telling me the hijacking story and others about Radio Caroline and how he was planning to make a documentary film about John & Bobby Kennedy and Martin Luther King.

Simon, my son, was still down at the party with Tadgh keeping an eye on him. I popped down at one point to find Simon in the arms of a woman. He was a toddler at the time and partial to women who were showing large, exposed breasts. He regularly liked to be held by Oonagh in her low-cut dresses. As I didn't possess similar dresses, it was a novelty for him. Often Simon's little hand would stray down the front of the dress, much to Oonagh's amusement. I could see he was working up to doing the same thing that day. The woman claimed she was fine with him so I returned upstairs where Ronan suggested we adjourn to my bedsitting room. I thought it was because the noise from the party was echoing up the stairs into my kitchen and he wanted a quieter space for talking. He did want a quieter space, but not for talking and soon started trying to give me passionate kisses.

When I protested that I barely knew him and that it was a little premature for such actions, he claimed he felt like he'd known me for years. I laughed, believing it was another of his chat-up lines.

We were disturbed with Tadgh returning Simon to me. He'd been up to his old tricks and Oonagh thought he'd grabbed enough breasts for one day. That soon put an end to Ronan's passion.

I had my own phone connected in the flat and Ronan asked me for my number. I didn't expect to hear from him again. I was wrong. He rang the following week and asked me out to dinner. I put him off a few times and then eventually agreed to it.

I arranged a babysitter and drove to meet him at a restaurant near Brompton Road somewhere. I wanted to pay for my own meal in case he had the same view I'd encountered with Australian men. They believed if they paid for the meal you 'owed' them sexual favours. He was surprised at my insistence and agreed, then suggested we went back to his place in Chelsea for coffee. I went (for tea – I don't drink coffee). Although the evening ended with some passion, it didn't work for me. I'd found some of his behaviour strange and overly paranoid. I liked Ronan but I wasn't attracted to him in that way. We talked and agreed when we met again it would be as 'friends'. He said he would like to continue seeing me as we got on so well, however other things intervened in the meantime.

Oonagh split up with her husband Sonny and asked me to let him have my 'flat'. She wanted me to move into Tadgh's bedroom upstairs and then share common areas with her and Tadgh. Tadgh was to move into the guest bedroom/study extension built onto the rear of the her flat. I didn't have much choice in the matter, otherwise I would have been homeless. She and Sonny remained on good terms though and he joined us for meals every night. It was at this point Sonny taught me how to make an 'Indian' style curry using different

12

spices rather than curry powder. Another thing I am very grateful for – I have been making 'curry' meals ever since. Sonny's family was Parsee from Karachi and had had to flee after partition. He'd attended university in England, qualifying as an architect (and would later become involved with Ronan in Caroline Homes). The rest of his family emigrated to Canada at some point.

Fed up with how difficult it was to find accommodation with a child I was keen to buy my own place. I'd taken on extra night work at a local Disco to save money. Oonagh used to babysit, or if she wanted to go out, I'd pay someone to come in and look after both our children. Sometimes Sonny would babysit. I was saving as much as I could every month.

At this point Oonagh was talking about selling the one-bedroom flat on the top floor of her house and Sonny and I discussed how that would work for me long term as Simon grew. He suggested a loft conversion. Oonagh was away in France doing some French courses while we discussed this option but, on her return, she was not happy about the possibility of a loft conversion in the future so wouldn't let me buy the flat. She'd talked about asking £8000 for it which was a little too expensive for me anyway. I soon found another one bedroomed flat for £6500 and applied to the local authority for a mortgage. In those days they were one of the easier options for obtaining finance for house purchases.

Oonagh kept pushing me to hurry the sale through as she had a few new French friends she wanted to come over to stay with her. My seller was also putting pressure on me. He said he had a cash buyer lined up if I didn't hurry matters along.

The day I was due to move into the new flat I was at work with all my belongings when my solicitor phoned saying the sale had fallen though. I couldn't understand how that had happened as we'd exchanged contracts and were completing that day. Apparently, a clerk at Camden Council had been dealing with last minute details and decided it was an illegal sale so cancelled everything. My solicitor, not being a conveyancing expert, accepted it. There I was at work, homeless.

My boss found me crying in the stock cupboard and after discovering what had happened phoned Camden Council to give them the sharp end of his tongue. He claimed they should have realised the legal aspects sooner and as a result were responsible for making me homeless. They agreed to put me in a B & B.

A few days later it was discovered that the clerk at the council was wrong. He'd been looking at the ground rent act of 1968. It had been amended in 1969. Unfortunately, the flat owner had proceeded with the cash buyer once he'd been told the sale had collapsed. Money had exchanged hands and the new buyer had already moved in despite legal paperwork not being completed. It was too late for me. Not only that but he had the right to keep the deposit I'd put down because I'd defaulted on the contract.

Eventually half of my deposit was returned – many weeks later. Within days the council put me onto a Housing Association and I moved into a very large one bedroomed flat on the edge of West Hampstead/ Kilburn. It was short-life property in poor condition so when I eventually received my deposit back it went into making the flat more presentable. It is said in life that things happen for a reason. If I hadn't lost the flat, I doubt I would ever have become involved with Ronan's different projects, nor followed other paths.

Ronan, meanwhile had been trying to reach me at Oonagh's and eventually found out I'd moved. I had a new telephone installed in the Housing Association flat and he was one of my first callers. When I told him what happened and the state of the place I'd been housed in, he offered his spare bedroom to Simon and me. It was typical of his generosity. If he had something he could give, he did. I mentioned Ronan's offer to Oonagh and she said he once gave his spare bedroom to two little old men, who ended up living there with him for years (but they routinely fed Ronan, apparently providing him with tasty meals).

I thanked Ronan and told him I planned to stay where I was. He suggested I should start working for him, but I told him I had a day job and extra work at nights over the weekend so I didn't have the time.

I had a background in classical and modern ballet from Australia and had hoped to break into that world in the UK. The macho Aussie journalists I lived with briefly in WC2 put paid to that idea. I was too short to gain a spot in ballet companies as they had height restrictions of 5'5" to 5'8". I was only 5'2". Dougie Squires Second Generation group was the only dance troupe that didn't have height requirements. I obtained an audition with them, but the men at the Aussie house decided they wouldn't let me go. They had this warped view that dancers became 'sluts' and didn't want to see that happen to me. They also didn't believe it was the right kind of life for a young child to be dragged all over the country without a settled home. I thought that while Simon was young it was manageable. As he grew, I knew that wouldn't be the case, but hoped to have made inroads into the industry by then to find a London based job.

The men locked me into my room in the house and hid all my dance gear (leotards, tights etc) so that I couldn't attend the audition. I was furious as it was my only chance. These men used to sit and watch Top of the Pops every week and when Pan's People came on, they'd be calling out 'slut', 'whore' to the women in the dance group. I never understood it and no amount of arguing with them would make them change their minds.

When my potential dance career disappeared out of the window, I began thinking of other options. In 1972 I had landed a job with IPC Magazines, as part of a team in the 'Offers' section, doing the reader's special offers in Woman's Own, Ideal Home and Woman's Journal. I considered a writing career – becoming a features writer in the magazine division. I was already a proficient typist. As a teenager I'd taught myself on a typewriter my grandmother gave me together with an ancient typing exercise book. IPC sent me on a new speedwriting course which was held for an hour each weekday. I had to sacrifice my lunch hour to attend it. However, I soon realised from my trips into the different magazines that this was a cut-throat world where you had to start at the bottom and I couldn't see it fitting in with a young child. I was offered a sub-editor's job on Woman's Own where you had to work until 8pm two nights a week. As it wouldn't have fitted my life with Simon, I declined the offer and remained with the Offers Department.

Next, I considered going to university and studying for a history degree. I had been studying A level History at home of an evening. But I decided I'd miss the dance part of my life too much. The ideal solution was to combine my two loves, history and dance. I could teach them at secondary level. As I no longer had to worry about paying a mortgage, I applied for teacher-training college. My qualifications from school in Australia weren't recognised, so I had to sit a 'Special Entry' examination at London University. Following further tests in English and Maths at the college campus, I was offered a place to start at Southland's College in Wimbledon in late September 1974. I would be studying history and dance at a degree equivalent level. I didn't realise at the time that these courses didn't hold the same kudos as a History degree would have.

The college placement offer I received was dependent on my gaining some experience with young teenagers that I had to report back on. I began volunteering with West Hampstead Action Committee (WHAC) while still at IPC but then decided to pack in that job in the spring of '74 so I could become more involved in activities and meetings with WHAC. WHAC were a voluntary group dealing with young people who had been permanently excluded from secondary school. I spent a few days a week on WHAC work, picked up temporary bookkeeping work and also continued with the evening work I had already been doing for some years, although at a different location by this time. I know there's no point in looking back over life and regretting decisions we make, but I often wished I'd remained at IPC until starting college or made different choices. 1974 turned out to be the worst year of my life – especially the months between March and September. It would take several chapters to explain it all and it is not particularly relevant to my Caroline journey, so I will not do so here. For those who might be interested I will add appendix chapters where I relate those experiences. It encompasses a social era that one hopes is no longer present today.

Back in the 70s there were grants available for higher education. The Greater London Council (GLC) offered me a grant of £13 per week and all college fees paid for. At the time I thought I was so lucky to be receiving it, but it didn't provide me with enough to cover all my costs so I had to find work. What I didn't realise was that the GLC were not giving me any allowances for Simon. They also failed to tell me that there was a division in Social Security that would give students like me a child allowance of £6.50 a week – throughout the year. I didn't find this out until well into my third year. Of course, they wouldn't backdate it, so I lost a considerable amount of money due to the prejudices the GLC had towards 'unmarried' mothers. My friend Brenda enrolled in North London University to do a degree in the autumn of 1977 following the completion of my course in June the same year. She was to receive a grant of £55 per week from the GLC against the approximate £20 I received the year prior. Because she had been *married* and had a young child, the GLC paid her the full grant. Years later (in the early 80s) when a friend of mine became a member of the first Women's Committee formed at the GLC, I approached her and asked her to find out whether the GLC still had this policy towards unmarried mothers. They did. The committee took the case up. The GLC bombarded them with documents that must have been almost a foot high, justifying their reasons for this discrimination and refusing to make any changes. It was unbelievable. When grants came to an end under Tony Blair in the 90s, it was no longer relevant. I wonder how many people's lives were affected by this discrimination; how many women were unable to undertake a higher education course due to being offered such low grants. Some wouldn't have been able to face the challenges. I almost didn't start the journey as I knew it was going to be tough. But after emerging from the horrors I encountered in the months, weeks and days prior to my course starting, it was one of the main things that kept me going. I was determined.

Once I started college, I took a job three nights a week at the Nomad Club in Paddington. They had a hostel above the club which largely catered to Australian, New Zealand and South African backpackers. I worked on reception three nights a week where during the hours of 7 – 11 pm all was quiet so I was able to study and work on essays. At 11pm the basement club came to life until 2am when I knocked off. When the snack bar franchise in the club became available, I applied for that offering club goers, burgers, lamb kebabs or toasted sandwiches on Thursday, Friday and Saturday Nights. That meant I was working six nights a week.

After splitting up with her partner, my friend Brenda had moved into my short life flat with her five-year-old daughter Claudia. Brenda babysat while I worked on the reception job. I hired a babysitter for the other three nights so Brenda could work in the snack bar with me. It was tough. I would rise at 7 am and get Simon ready for nursery. Then head off to college for the day. Back home after college I would feed and bathe the two children and put them to bed before heading off to my evening job. I was lucky if I had four hours sleep a night. On Thursday mornings I rose several hours earlier to travel to Smithfield meat market where I bought meat for the snack bar at wholesale prices.

Ronan called me for a quick chat every so often – usually over the weekend – and every time we spoke, he tried to persuade me to work for him. I hadn't told him anything about my nightmare months that year. With my busy schedule I had little available time. Saturday during the day was for shopping, housework and time with the kids. Sunday was for the kids and study in the evening. But with no lectures on a Friday afternoon I eventually said, 'Okay I can offer you Friday afternoons.'

3

Ronan asked me to call in to his flat on my return from college the following Friday afternoon after I agreed to join his workforce. It was an easy diversion to Chelsea on my journey from Wimbledon, where the college was located, to where I had just moved to in South Hampstead. The short life property I had been living in in West Hampstead was due to be demolished so the council re-housed me in a basement/garden flat a short distance away in South Hampstead. It was also only a one bedroom flat – but with large rooms, Sonny (Oonagh's husband) later helped me to split the bedroom into two.

The particular project that convinced me to work for Ronan was the Kennedy/King movie. He knew I was interested in the three icons (Jack and Bobby Kennedy and Martin Luther King) and I was intrigued as to what he thought I could contribute to the film.

After ringing his bell, there was a delay at the flat entrance, one that was to become a standard procedure in ensuing years. Ronan would only admit visitors or bell ringers if he recognised them. This necessitated a discreet peeping out of the curtains to ascertain who was there. He didn't always answer to those he knew either. Not unless he was expecting them. He didn't appreciate unexpected visitors.

Ronan's raised ground floor flat was essentially a square box. A hallway ran down the middle of it; to the left there was a small galley kitchen (which had a door that opened on to a small exterior yard surrounded by the flats), a bathroom and the second double bedroom. To the right, which faced the road at the front, was the lounge and the larger bedroom.

When I arrived at his flat, I was introduced to a man called Chris Moore. I recall him being a quiet, dark haired, good looking giant of a man who towered over both Ronan and I.

'I want you, Chris and Oonagh to be the directors of a film company,' Ronan said. He had paperwork all ready for Chris and I to sign.

The Company was to be called 'Research Educational Systems Limited (Films Branch UK)'. I naively asked Ronan what other branches the company had.

He looked at me with a confused expression and then once it dawned on him, he burst out laughing. 'You're joking?' he asked. I wasn't. The name implied that there were other branches to Research Educational Systems. I wasn't familiar with Ronan's way of operating at the time. Of course, there were no other branches. I don't know who came up with this unwieldy name for the company – he might have bought a company 'off the shelf'. With the name being a bit of a mouthful, myself and other

23

staff tended to shorten it to Research Educational Films (hereafter referred to as REF) in subsequent years when communicating verbally with film laboratories or other companies.

'What would you expect us to do as directors of this film company?'

'Chris won't be doing anything, Ronan said. 'He will simply sign papers each year for the company returns. Oonagh might have some involvement but you will be the main active director.'

This surprised me. 'And what would I be doing?'

'Placing official orders for footage, dealing with the accounts – you're a qualified bookkeeper aren't you (yes I was from earlier training in Australia in the years after I left school and I had imparted this information to Ronan in one of our previous meetings), paying bills, – you will need to open a bank account to deal with those and paying the staff wages every Friday afternoon. I'll tell you about them in a minute.'

And here he snuck in another little task. 'But before you go and pay them on Fridays, I would also like you to rotate around all the record companies each Friday afternoon to collect new album releases that we can send out to the ship. It wouldn't take you long to do that – you don't have to go the same ones every week.'

So, he wanted me to do work for Radio Caroline as well. Something he'd been angling at for more than a year.

'How does that work then?' I asked him.

'I'll give you the names of all the A & R guys you

need to make contact with and they will give you the new releases.'

'Make contact with them by phone?'

'Yes, you'll need to mention you're collecting the records for Radio Caroline.'

'Call them at my own expense?' I asked him. He knew I always had a phone connected wherever I lived so that I could keep in touch with my family in Australia. It was not cheap though and I was a student, plus I was out most days during working office hours. I thought this was going to prove difficult. I had an aversion to public phones and hated using them after being unexpectedly and brutally assaulted by some older teenage girls while I was using one at the age of 11. It was both comical and tragic watching me attempt to use one. It could prove problematic for this task.'How much are you going to pay me for this?' I asked him.

'I can give you £10 each Friday for your work. I will give you the odd extra tenner to cover petrol and other expenses.'

It seemed reasonable. I looked at the paperwork he placed before me and noticed my name had been written as L. Gilbert. Chris was listed as C. Moore, Oonagh's as O. Leigh (her former married name).

'Why not my full name?' I asked.

'There's no need to put first names or middle names and their initials,' he said.

I shrugged, not realising that there was another agenda linked to his reasoning for this. An agenda I wasn't to discover for some years.

Included in the paperwork was a contract from a company in Lichtenstein who would transfer money from there directly into the bank account which he wanted me to open. It gave a breakdown of the role REF would play in making the film on behalf of the Lichtenstein company and what it would receive in return for doing so. I can't recall all of those details, but I believe REF was to receive a percentage of all the profits once the film was released and had sole distribution rights for the UK. Not all the forms could be completed that day as the registered address had to be decided upon. Subsequently the registered office was located at Gray's Inn – with the company's accountants I believe. Oonagh's and my telephone number were listed on the letterhead I had printed. All this changed a few years later. That first day though, Ronan simply wanted Chris and I to sign and we were asked to leave it undated.

Once the paperwork was signed Chris left us. Ronan told me that Chris had been one of the early 'jocks' on Caroline back in the 60s. I couldn't gauge how close their friendship was as Chris spoke only a few words the whole time I was in his presence.

Ronan then went on to tell me that the film was already in full swing. The working title of the film was 'The K Index'. He had a director called Dick Fontaine. An editor called Tim L___ and a researcher called David. He didn't know David's surname (and I've forgotten it now). From time to time, he also engaged (or possibly Dick did on Ronan's behalf) researchers in the USA who were attempting to track down witnesses to John

Kennedy's assassination.

After dealing with numerous phone calls and several cups of tea later, I drove Ronan over to meet the film crew and see the set-up they had there. It was in a maisonette over two floors located in 16 Elvaston Place SW7. We entered the apartment on the lower floor into the living room which was painted in greens and golds with thick velvet curtains.

'Jimmy Hendrix once lived here,' Ronan told me. 'This is still his décor. Heavy isn't it?'

'It's not the flat he died in, is it?' I asked.

'No,' he said shaking his head, but not elaborating.

I followed him up to another floor by an internal staircase where the rooms were much lighter – either painted white or had light wallpaper. A large front room was set up as an office with desks and cabinets where Dick worked. Next to it was a cutting room where Tim worked. It was a long narrow room with a *Steenbeck* editing machine.

I watched as Tim cut and spliced both film and sound tapes, re-joining them seamlessly. What he'd then altered could be played back on the small screen in front of him. The process fascinated me and I was to spend endless hours in the years that followed taking note of how it was all achieved.

Tim was friendly and welcomed me. Dick gave me a cursory nod of greeting and asked to speak to Ronan privately. David wasn't there. I would meet him another day.

While Ronan was talking to Dick, I asked Tim a number

of questions and learned that they were working on part one of the film. Although it was a documentary film, Ronan wanted it released in cinemas as any blockbuster film would be. He believed the subject matter was too important to be wasted on a television documentary.

Tim played me the opening sequences which started with Marvin Gaye's song, *Abraham, Martin and John*, interspersed with rockets taking off and other real footage of JFK, Martin Luther King and Bobby Kennedy – the last one mentioned in the song. All assassinated politicians.

It seemed exciting and something I would be interested to be involved with. I believed the Caroline aspect of my work for Ronan would be incidental. How wrong I was.

Collecting the records every Friday became a regular routine. Back in those days it was easy to drive around and park in the West End where many of the record companies were based. Armed initially with a *London A – Z*, I would weave my way around the narrow streets and in no time at all I knew all the short-cuts and rat runs to reach my destinations quicker. I joked with friends that I could take the 'knowledge' exam that black cab drivers had to pass. There were a number of companies outside the West End. I can't recall all of them now. But Chrysalis and Island Records were two of them. I did a separate run for the West London companies, avoiding the West End on those days. The record companies often gave me multiple copies of every album, which included they said, a couple of additional copies for me to keep for my personal use. My record collection starting growing when I kept back these additional records by artists I liked. I would open and play one of them and keep a second copy in pristine condition.

David, our film researcher asked if he could join

me on these runs when his work was slack and we subsequently became good friends. Once the Nomad Club I worked in closed down, and I didn't have to rush home to sort the kids and head off for work, I would often join Tim and David for early Friday evening drinks at the pub. I only had a couple, but I would drive home without giving it a second thought. We all did it in those days.

I don't remember who I dropped the records off to, possibly Oonagh as she travelling back and forth to the continent. In the second half of 1975 Ronan asked me to start taking them across to France for the tenders. 1975 also saw the increase of the time he asked me to put into both Radio Caroline and the film.

One of the first additional tasks Ronan asked me to perform was to collect a large sum of money from Amsterdam. He claimed he had a friendly bank manager there who channelled the money through his bank from Lichtenstein, the main base where funds were sent.

I never asked Ronan where the money came from. I assumed some of it was from advertising on Caroline, although there weren't many advertisements in the 70s, with it being illegal by then. He did tell me though that the owners of the Mi Amigo radio station which was also based on the ship, contributed funds so I made an assumption that they were paying a hefty whack.

Ronan always referred to them as a 'Dutch' station and so that was how we all came to think of Radio Mi Amigo. It was years later that I discovered that the founder of Radio Mi Amigo was in fact a successful

Belgium (Flemish) businessman called Sylvain Tack. Most of the DJs were Dutch and the station was hugely popular across Belgium, the Netherlands, and Luxembourg.

Ronan told me it was illegal to bring large sums of cash into the UK or leave countries with so much money. He said I had to find an ingenious way to hide the money on me to get it through customs. I did think of something very simple and it worked every time. I would ask the bank to provide me with the largest notes they could which I redistributed throughout my bag in a particular way. It was hidden in plain sight – if the customs officials bothered to look more closely. Despite my bag being emptied out and searched on a number of occasions, they never found the money.

The first run I did wasn't as large as subsequent ones. I think it was only about £10,000. I travelled to Amsterdam on 18th April 1975. Although I have a good memory for dates, I wouldn't necessarily recall precise dates that far back. I checked out my old passport which has pages of stamps from when I left the country. There were inconsistencies with the stamping of my passport though. Generally, when I flew, it would be stamped by English Customs at Heathrow – on my exit and return. Countries such as France and Switzerland, never stamped my passport upon arrival or departure. Other European countries I visited (eg Greece) stamped it. The Netherlands stamped it on arrival and departure. When travelling to France by ferry, English customs *usually* stamped it on leaving the country and returning.

The stamps from British Customs was because I had an Irish Passport at the time. When I left Australia to come to the UK, I obtained the Irish passport (through my grandparents) that would enable me to remain indefinitely in the UK rather than being restricted by a grumpy customs officer that might only grant me three months stay. I'd been warned by Australian friends that it was a lottery on the amount of time Australians would be granted to remain in the country back then. You had to leave the UK before your time expired and then return again, hoping for a more generous official that would grant you a longer stay next time around. Things are done differently today.

As the 70s progressed I would be looked up on lists of names to see if I was linked to the IRA. At some point British Customs ceased stamping my passport on every trip and after obtaining British citizenship in the 80s and gaining a British passport in the early 90s, English customs and other European countries ceased stamping my passport altogether. However, when I travelled to Europe this year (2022) I received my first ever stamp from French Customs – due to Brexit.

I do recall that the first trip to Amsterdam I made for Ronan was on a Friday and I would not have minded missing 'education' lectures that morning. I believe by then my Easter Holiday break from college was over.

With the Nomad Club closed by this time, I'd picked up a couple of evening shifts in the pub next door to the Nomad but when the publican moved that came to an end. I had to grab as much other work as I could. During the Easter break that year I worked as a temporary cook in my son's nursery. In the long summer holidays that year, I joined an agency and picked up work as an auditor in the West End several days a week. Working for Ronan was squeezed in around the time I had free.

On my trips to collect money in the Netherlands I would fly out in the morning and might return in the evening or late at night. Looking back now, I think that first trip was a test run to see if I was honest and brought all the money back to him. He sent me again on 28th April and I returned with £25,000. It necessitated taking a larger handbag.

In 1975 Ronan was sharing his flat with a woman called Maria. As far as I was concerned, they were a couple – Ronan referred to Maria in a way a partner would if she was his girlfriend. Maria had decorated the back bedroom and claimed she preferred to sleep in there. The ceiling was painted navy blue and she'd placed stars on it that shone when the lights were turned off.

I didn't think there was anything strange about Maria having her own bedroom. An ex-Caroline staff member argued that having separate rooms showed they weren't a couple. He believed they were always just friends as Ronan was still chatting up other women as often as he could. But Ronan never stopped being a flirt around women and many couples like to have their own rooms. I've insisted on it the few times I've lived with a partner – where possible. Men often have studies, or their 'man caves' which is a similar principle. And perhaps the fact that Ronan had flings with other women was why the relationship didn't last long term (although Maria was there for some years). Whatever the status of their relationship was, Maria was pivotal in providing support and encouragement to Ronan and his enterprises in the 70s. She was the woman behind the man. Or one of the key ones, I should say.

The trips to Amsterdam meant I would be away the whole day and sometimes I couldn't pick up a flight to return until the evening. Ronan suggested that I leave my son Simon with him and Maria on my second trip; which of course, would also ensure my return. I didn't see it like that at the time, but I am sure that was part of his agenda. The two of them looking after Simon proved so successful, they offered to do it every time I did a run. Or I should say Ronan made the offer – whether he discussed it with Maria first I don't know. I didn't always take them up on this offer but they looked after Simon a number of times. If I returned late, Simon would be put to bed in Maria's room and a bedtime story read to him from one of the books I'd leave with them. Simon became enamoured with the dark ceiling and stars and so eventually I had to decorate his bedroom like that – in several places where we lived. Once I returned, I would lift my sleeping child into my car and drive home.

At some point that year Ronan introduced me to Ernst. Ernst was a lawyer from Lichtenstein who handled Ronan's affairs. Because of the money runs I did and the film company Ronan wanted me to get to know Ernst more. Usually, he kept people in separate compartments with never the twain meeting. Ernst was an easy-going guy with a sense of humour so I asked him whether he would be willing to be my cover for the runs. I hadn't been asked yet, but I knew the day would come when a customs officer would ask me why I was travelling back and forth to Amsterdam on the same day so often. I planned to say it was for business meetings but I doubted that would work. I didn't look like a businesswoman.

I told Ernst that I could tell any Customs official who enquired that I had a wealthy boyfriend who was based in Europe, and that I would fly over to join him for sex and a meal, then return home. If push came to shove could I give his name? He agreed but it was some years before I needed to use the 'plausible' story.

Twice in the years that followed I had to make a trip to Lichtenstein instead of Amsterdam as the money couldn't be sent through for some reason. I flew into Zurich before heading to Lichtenstein. I can't recall how I travelled there from Zurich – perhaps by train or bus. Customs officials at Zurich airport were very strict and carried out strip searches on departure.

I met Ernst both times and his wife and young son on one trip, joining them for lunch in their home. Whilst there I opened a bank account in Lichtenstein with Ernst's help with the Verwaltungs-UND Privat Bank. Oonagh had been working for Ronan again for some years by this time and I knew that she had opened an account there and part of her wages were deposited in it every week. I thought Ronan could do the same for me, but he refused to so the low opening deposit I gave Ernst (I believe it was only £5) only ever increased through interest. I often think about that account and still have the paperwork relating to it. I know some banks close accounts after many years of inactivity and I've often wondered if the bank did that with mine. The last statement I received from Ernst in 1989 showed a balance of 29.45 (although I have no idea what currency it referred to).

The number of hours I was putting into both Radio Caroline and the film seemed to be increasing month by month. Ronan and I argued over the Lichtenstein account. He'd promised me an increase in wages and I couldn't see why he couldn't put money into an account for me there like he did for Oonagh.

'I've got so many expenses – people to pay, I can't do it at the moment,' he claimed. 'However, I am willing to bung you a large lump sum at some point if there's something special you want to save for.'

I still had aspirations of buying my own place one day. It simply wasn't feasible while I was still a student.

'Okay …,' I said, not sure whether his word could be trusted as he wasn't keeping his promise to pay me more. 'I do want to buy my own place one day. Perhaps when I'm ready you could pay a substantial deposit towards it and my purchasing fees.'

'Of course,' he said and seemed delighted with this result. Years later this would be put to the test. But that's for another time.

5

One of the additional tasks Ronan asked me to do for
Caroline was to listen to audition tapes with Oonagh. He
thought two judgements on the viability of a potential
presenter was better than one. I'm not sure what address
these tapes were sent to back in those days. We did have
an address in Rosas, Girona, Spain, which was operated
by a friend of Oonagh's. They may have gone there and
then found their way back to her place in London. I know
we listened to most of them at Oonagh's house. The two
of us generally agreed on which ones we might hire and
she would contact them to make an appointment for us
to interview them.

I wasn't party to the hiring of 'James Ross' though. He
first went out to Caroline in June 1975 under a different
name and I was to meet him at Ronan's that year when
Ronan asked us to carry out a particular task. Our first
meeting might have been before James went out to the
ship.

Ronan phoned me and asked me to drop over to his
flat. When I arrived, there was the usual delay while he

checked who was at the door.

'Morning,' he said. 'Come through, there's someone I want you to meet.'

He took me through to the living room and introduced me to a young man sitting there. He had long hair past his shoulders and seemed very shy as he barely looked at us.

He introduced me as 'Liz' which I thought was strange and he gave me, what I was to later learn, the young man's real name. I wasn't sure why he'd used a false name for me.

'Liz is involved in running things behind the scenes,' Ronan told him.

The young man nodded and smiled.

'I have a little job I'd like you both to do for me.'

'Oh, what's that?' I asked Ronan.

'We're doing a promotion of Elton John's new album on Caroline. I want you two to go up to Sheffield to buy it, or order it from as many shops as you can.'

'I doubt we could do that in one day,' I said. 'Are you expecting me to drive up in my car?'

'Yes. I'll pay for overnight accommodation and expenses. I've asked Oonagh to find the names of all the record shops in Sheffield as well as a hotel for you. There are small teams like yours going out across the country to do this.'

'And if we have to order it, how will that work? They might not have it in stock for a week or so. Do you expect us to go back?'

'No. I'll have someone else do that. The most

important thing is to pay for it so it registers as a sale.'

'Is his record company paying you to do this?' I asked him. 'I saw Elton John last week when I popped into Sony records down in Soho on Friday afternoon. He was getting into the lift with a couple of men, looking like he'd not long surfaced after partying all night. I can't imagine that an album of Elton John's needs extra promotion.'

'Apparently it's not doing too well at the moment. This is a favour for a friend.' He didn't explain who the friend was.

'Right,' I said nodding.

'Liz collects all the music for Caroline,' Ronan said turning to James, 'and often bumps into recording artists while she's on her rounds.'

'I wouldn't use the word "often". I've only ever seen a few.'

'Right. Back to business,' Ronan continued. 'I'd like you to go next Saturday. Will that be possible?'

'I'd have to take Simon with me – if that's okay, I could do it then.'

Ronan nodded.

'That's not a problem. What about you?' he asked the young man.

'Yes, next weekend is fine for me,' he said.

'That's settled then. I'll leave you two to make arrangements for meeting up. I have some calls to make,' Ronan said handing me a pile of cash. We were being dismissed.

* * *

James turned up at my place early the following Saturday. He seemed surprised when I introduced him to Simon. I realised neither I, nor Ronan, had explained that Simon was a boy less than four years old.

'Did you think Simon was going to be my boyfriend?' I asked him.

'I … I didn't know who he … yes maybe, or he might have been a friend.'

'Okay. I've packed sandwiches and drinks for us. Let's hit the road.'

'How long have you been working for Ronan?' James asked me as I turned onto the M1 Motorway.

'I started working for him last Autumn – towards the second half of Autumn,' I added.

'Apart from listening to audition tapes and collecting the records for Caroline, what else do you do?'

The quiet shy young man I'd met at Ronan's the week before had turned into a chatty, inquisitive young man. And there I'd been thinking we'd probably have little conversation on the journey.

'I travel to Europe to collect the wages for the DJs and crew. I've never done this sort of thing before. I mean this trip to Sheffield. I'm also involved in running a company on behalf of Ronan where we're making a film about John and Bobby Kennedy and Martin Luther King. It's a documentary film.'

'What do you do on that?

I filled him in on my Friday afternoon ritual and work I might take home with me.

He was silent for a bit before asking, 'How does the record thing work? I mean the record companies are giving you records that are intended for a pirate radio station. Isn't it illegal?'

'It's not illegal to give a young woman or man a collection of records. They could always claim they don't know what I do with them. I have no idea what they log in their official records – if they log anything. They know they're for Caroline though. I have contacts in all the companies. They're happy to give them to us. It means their artists are played on the air which in turn means people will buy them. We get free music and they make sales. Everyone's happy.'

We chatted on an off all the way to Sheffield. Once there, I drove to the hotel where we'd be staying and left our overnight bags there. Back then there was no such thing as a Sat Nav (not that I've ever used one – but many of my friends do and follow them slavishly). The hotel had sent a small map to help me find it. I've always been good with maps and I found it easily enough. The hotel then gave us maps of the city. After dumping our bags, we split up and went off to the different stores, agreeing to meet back at the hotel later. We did have to order the album in some stores and collected order slips confirming it had been paid for to take back to Ronan.

We ate our evening meal at the hotel and then I went off to bathe Simon and put him to bed with a story. The friendly receptionist suggested I could safely leave Simon alone in our (mine and Simon's) room as they had child monitors that could be switched on. Once he was asleep, I switched the monitor on and went back down to the receptionist and requested she put her end of the monitor on. I sat in the lounge near the reception to have a glass of wine, followed by a pot of tea. I knew I would be able to hear if any noise came through the monitor. James joined me and we chatted.

At about 9pm the female receptionist went off duty and was replaced by a man who I thought was rather creepy. I don't think he realised the 'child monitor' was on.

The man disappeared and a short while later I heard Simon through the monitors screaming and crying out. I'm also sure I heard a door slam shut. I raced upstairs to our room, bumping into the male receptionist/night porter coming down looking flushed.

'What's going on?' I asked him.

He claimed he didn't know what I was talking about.

Once in the room I turned the monitor off and gathered Simon into my arms. He was distressed and crying. I wondered if he'd had a bad dream – although it would have been unusual. Simon was a heavy sleeper and it took a lot to wake him. He also wasn't one to cry easily. When I asked him what was wrong, he kept saying over and over, 'The man was trying to hurt me.'

I couldn't get any other sense out of him. He was too distressed to explain exactly what 'the man' was attempting to do to him. I checked him over and he seemed physically fine. I switched the monitor back on once Simon settled back into sleep and went downstairs to challenge the receptionist. He claimed he hadn't been in our room and didn't know what I was talking about. I didn't believe him though. He was a shifty character. James was still there looking concerned. I told him what had happened and that I thought it best if I retired for the night.

In the morning I raised the issue with yet another receptionist who seemed at a loss as to what could have happened. To me it was obvious. The night receptionist had gone into our room, either to check on Simon and startled him, or had attempted to do something to him. The receptionist thought it unlikely and claimed it wasn't part of his job to do anything like that. It might not have been part of his job but I'm sure that's what happened. We checked out and returned to London.

I phoned Ronan on my return and confirmed our mission had been accomplished. I also told him about the incident with Simon.

The following Friday I handed Ronan the order slips which he put to one side. I suspect those orders were never collected. Showing concern, he asked me how Simon was.

'He's woken, distressed, a few times in the past week shouting about the man trying to hurt him,' I said. In fact, Simon had nightmares for several more weeks following that incident.

'Don't ever ask me to do anything like that again,' I told him.

43

6

The next time I was to see James was many months later at my flat. This time it was to collect his wages. Ronan had asked me to start handing out the presenters' (or 'Jocks' as he called them) wages to them when they returned. Previously I had passed the money on to Oonagh or simply left the money with Ronan. He paid some of the 'Caroline' staff himself. There were a handful of presenters I never met as they dealt directly with him. It was the same with the engineers.

In September 1975 my timetable at college altered so that I only had to attend lectures two and a half days a week. This remained in place until my course finished in June 1977. I began looking around for other work that didn't necessitate me having to go out to work in the evenings. I obtained a bookkeeping job that I did on Monday afternoons for an import/export company. That job lasted for about a year. I also took on another bookkeeping job all day Wednesday. The Wednesday job was with an expanding company that made toiletry bags. Taking on this job kept me going financially for many years. During college holidays I would put in more hours with the company.

Friday afternoons were still devoted to Caroline and the film. I was also putting in many hours of work at home of an evening or over weekends for Radio Caroline or the film. On the film front I might have to type a letter to a film laboratory asking what footage they might have relevant to our story. I might then request a contract with a licence to use it with costings or purchase it outright. Our researcher David would often notify me of particular footage a company might have and then I would go straight into the contract, licence or purchase request. David didn't have a car and if it was in an awkward location, I would need to visit the laboratory, collect the relevant roll of film and deliver it to Elvaston Place.

On the Radio Caroline front, it was either paying wages to presenters, organising presenters or cooks to go out on the next tender, listening to tapes or liaising with Oonagh over some aspect of our work. When Oonagh was home (she was often in France) we spoke most days.

In December 1975 I had saved enough money from my various jobs for Simon and I to fly back to Australia to spend Christmas with my family. They had never met Simon until this trip – only seen him in photographs (Simon was born in Jersey, CI). Five days after returning from Australia I flew to Amsterdam on 9th January 1976 to collect money for Ronan.

On my return when he was sorting out money for

me to take home for the presenters pay, Ronan, out of the blue, asked me to take wages to his 'band'. Up until that point I had no idea he was supporting a band. He explained that he had been funding a band for some time (a couple of years I believe he told me) and they were soon going to record an album. He was moulding them into writing and playing in a style he wanted. I knew that in the past he'd managed various artists. I asked him what the name of the band was and he told me he hadn't decided yet. Their name was going to be his prerogative. I thought it all very strange.

He sent me to a space he rented for the band to rehearse where I met Charlie Charles, Norman Watt Roy, John Turnbull and Mick Gallagher – who were later to become part of the original 'Blockheads' who backed Ian Drury. But at this point they didn't have a name.

Charlie and I instantly hit it off and he started asking me to meet up with him. He told me he was married (to a Japanese woman I believe) with a young son, but the marriage was on the rocks. My first thoughts were, *that's what all married men say when trying to chat up a woman.*

But he didn't try to chat me up until he actually split with his wife. We went 'out' together to different music venues and he started coming around to see me at my flat. It was some months before we became involved in a brief romantic relationship.

Ronan didn't approve. Not because he had any interest in me. I believe he thought it might make me less available for work and distract Charlie from his rehearsals. It didn't. Other things distracted Charlie – his clubbing until all hours – and possibly drugs. I was told many years later that Charlie became a heroin addict and the band had to let him go. Back then I saw no sign of him taking drugs other than smoking and the odd drink.

Charlie was a lovely, generous guy. As a late birthday present in July 1976 he took me to the Proms. I'd mentioned that I'd always wanted to go to the Last Night of the Proms and he turned up at my place with surprise tickets – not for the last night. He'd bought tickets for a 'box' in Albert Hall. It was wonderful but I would have preferred to be standing with the crowd below. I found the 'box' location a little stuffy and confining. Charlie and I giggled every time one of our fellow box members or adjoining box members gave us sneering looks. I suspect they considered we weren't dressed appropriately or had racist thoughts about Charlie. They were all a white crowd dressed in evening wear.

The band recorded their album in Palm Springs, in the USA. They filmed a video of the single 'Love You To Know' at Stonehenge. I believe it was one of the earlier music videos made and we all thought it was excellent.

Ronan assembled the band, the film crew and other people associated with him at St. Thomas More Primary School for the album photo. I was there but after some hours I had to leave to pick up Simon. I can't recall why he wasn't there with me that day as most of the others had their children with them and it was a school holiday. Perhaps I wasn't told children could participate. When the proofs came through Ronan chose one that was taken after I left. I asked him for copies of earlier shots taken that I was in and he promised to get me some, but they were never forthcoming.

Ronan planned to launch the band and their album in Amsterdam with a large press conference which would be held simultaneously with one in New York where Lady Victoria Plumb (one of Ronan's friends) was meeting with the press at the World Trade Centre.

He still hadn't revealed what he was going to call them. They were getting mighty fed up with this and had over time put forward some suggestions themselves. All of which Ronan rejected. Just before the launch I asked Ronan if he had decided on a name for them. He said he had but refused to say what it was.

Ronan made copies of the single available for all of us but withheld the albums. The records were on a 'More Love Records' label based in the Netherlands. It was either another of Ronan's set up 'companies' or one he'd persuaded someone over there to fund. The single didn't have the name of the band on the record sleeve. The albums were withheld from us until the press conference where Ronan said all would be revealed.

Ronan asked me to travel to Amsterdam with him and the band for the launch. When I asked him why, he said he thought I might be needed – but wouldn't elaborate. By this time, the relationship between Charlie and I had drawn to a close – although we remained close friends for many months after. Charlie had wanted to either get serious or call it quits. I couldn't understand why he'd want to have a serious relationship that might lead to another marriage (this is what he said he wanted) when he'd not long come out of one. We talked about it at length and I pointed out that our lifestyles clashed too much. I had to be up early weekday mornings, take Simon to nursery (he didn't start mainstream school until September that year) then either drive from West Hampstead (where Simon's nursery was) to Wimbledon for college, or go to work. He wanted to go clubbing (which I could only do of Friday or Saturday night if I had a babysitter) or – if he came around to mine, which he might do any night of the week, he'd want to stay up listening to music until all hours. I struggled with only a few hours' sleep a night. I'd gone through that in the autumn of 1974 and it proved too much for me. I wasn't prepared to give up college. He said he couldn't change his lifestyle, so our relationship altered to one of simply friendship where we saw each other at work related things or he might pop around for dinner before going out clubbing for the night. We still occasionally went out together. The 'great friends' part of our friendship lasted until Charlie found a new 'love'. He stopped coming around altogether which saddened me (but this was some months after the launch). When we did occasionally meet up, we were always friendly. I last saw him in 1982 when I bumped into him on the West Hampstead/Kilburn borders. We spent a few hours catching up before parting. At the time he told me he was living with an Australian nurse in Kilburn. He promised to come back to see me in a few weeks, but didn't and he hadn't left me an address or phone number. Sadly, he died of cancer in 1990.

Back in June 1976, Simon went to stay with my friend Brenda overnight and I was able to join Ronan for the Amsterdam trip.

He paid for a large group of us to stay at a hotel (the Hilton I believe).

Looking back at the stamps in my passport, the only one in 1976 where I am away overnight in Amsterdam is on 23rd to 24th June. If I was on a money run, I would return the same day, so I believe this was the date of the band's launch.

We met up with various Dutch personnel who were involved in Mi Amigo and possibly the record, partying at an apartment right on one of the canals. I was very impressed with a bed I spotted in one of the bedrooms when returning from the bathroom and asked if I could sketch it. I kept the sketch and some years later had a hand-crafted bed made to a similar design.

I can't recall where the press conference was held, but we were linked up with Lady Victoria in New York who had many press members with her. We were also linked to the press in London.

Music by the band was played in the background, including I believe the video taken at Stonehenge for the single. The band members and I all waited with baited breath to hear what Ronan intended to call them.

The Albums had either a white or a glossy black cover and the title 'Loving Awareness'. Loving Awareness had been Ronan's pet project on Radio Caroline for some time. I know several of the presenters were a little embarrassed about mentioning it on air. Recorded messages were made and played regularly to ease their discomfort. Ronan had this idea that everyone should be 'loving' towards each other. Instead of 'defensive'. He talked about it often with me and called it 'Loving Awareness' and 'Defensive Awareness,' – he shortened it to LA and DA in conversations. In his book *The Radio Caroline Bible*, Paul Rusling refers to the 'DA' as 'Destructive Awareness'. Ronan may have altered the 'D' from 'defensive' to 'destructive' at a later date, but he always quoted 'Defensive Awareness' to me.

The startling aspect of the album Ronan promoted that day was that they had a large diagonal removeable label stuck to them that in large print read 'THE BEATLES'. In very small print above it, it read, 'everyone says they sound like' and underneath THE BEATLES it read: 'what do you think?' In other words: 'everyone says they sound like THE BEATLES, what do you think?'

The small print wasn't noticeable until looked at closely. The words THE BEATLES stood out.

Inside the sleeve cover were a couple of posters with strange artwork where John F Kennedy, Martin Luther King and Mahatma Ghandi were woven in. One of the posters featured an image of the band members across the bottom. Across the top of the posters 'LOVING AWARENESS' featured in large print.

Members of the press gasped when Ronan made his announcement, as did the band members and I. Ronan intimated that he was planning to call them 'The Beatles'.

Comments were thrown at Ronan saying "You can't call this band the Beatles,"; "There will be legal repercussions"; "You will be sued by members of The Beatles" and similar comments. The press – and the band members, were angry with Ronan.

The press conference disintegrated amidst the protests, particularly after the reporters got wind of a major news story coming in. Research of major news items at the time show that Howard K. Smith, an ABC News Commentator, revealed that President Lyndon Johnson had told him that Fidel Castro was behind the assassination of John F. Kennedy. Johnson had claimed that "Kennedy was trying to get Castro, but Castro got him first." (Wikipedia is the only site that refers to this news item).

Our research into JFK's assassination on the film proved that this was not true and that in fact Cuban exiles, opposed to Castro, were part of the conspiracy. Kennedy had in fact been secretly reaching out to Castro attempting to reconcile the two countries and move towards peace. Something the Cuban exiles, the US military (and Johnson was a great supporter of the military), and the CIA didn't want.

The only other major news stories from the day before (23rd June) was that the oil barge NEPCO 140 spilled a large quantity of oil into the St. Lawrence seaway after running aground and that the CN Tower, the world's large free-standing structure opened in Toronto.

Any of these items would have distracted journalists from the what they considered the launch of an insignificant band who were attempting to cash in the Beatles' success.

I'm inclined to believe Johnson's revelation was the story that drew all the journalists away that day. Whatever it was, we weren't told – they just left to follow up on whatever the breaking story was. But given its significance to the work both Ronan and I were doing, I don't understand why it didn't come up in subsequent conversations we had.

Ronan and the band fell out over his little stunt and it was the beginning of the end for their relationship – although I believe they performed at various venues for a short time after the launch. The single, *Love You to Know* was resonant of the sound the Beatles had in their latter days. This was what Ronan had been pushing them towards. Ronan told me he had George Harrison's encouragement and support in this vein. Rumours later emerged that George Harrison funded the band. That was not true – it was Caroline income which covered their costs over the years – however around the same time George did apparently give Ronan £15,000 to 'help out'. What Ronan used that money for is unknown.

The album was released without the strips that said 'THE BEATLES' and they were called 'The Loving Awareness Band' by presenters – which they weren't happy about. Ronan had intended Loving Awareness to be the name of the album, not the group's name. Once again, he had not consulted with them about its title. The album was a minor success. Tracks were played on Caroline but I don't think other stations gave it much, if any, airplay.

The following year the band joined up with Ian Drury and became a major part of 'The Blockheads' (they weren't the only members of this band), going on to have enormous success.

I didn't think I had much to offer in the way of support to the band with Ronan's stunt. I simply urged them to avoid overreacting and to distance themselves from events. They relied on Ronan to support themselves and their families. Being too annoyed with Ronan to discuss it calmly with him, I returned to England following the disastrous press conference.

We (Ronan and I) subsequently exchanged words over his actions. I was one of the few people who would challenge him back in those days. I had nothing to lose. I didn't rely solely on him for my income. He thought he had done the 'right thing' and couldn't understand why the band couldn't 'trust' him. He also thought that having invested all this money in them, paid for the recording and the launch, that they should be able to make their own living from that point on. In principle he was right. However, he didn't seem to understand that he had damaged their careers with *The Beatles* stunt and any chance of major success for the single would be blocked by most radio stations. He admitted that he had always planned to call them *The Beatles* and knew he wouldn't get away with it for long (hence why he had the removable labels on the album). He believed that the publicity and furore it would generate would bring them great success. He thought they were going to be massive and that he would start to make back the money he'd invested in them tenfold. Money that could support Radio Caroline and his other projects. It wasn't to be.

7

Ronan and I had regular disagreements over the years. Our arguments seldom included raised voices (not until later years anyway) or name calling. Our politics clashed dramatically at times. Ronan considered himself an entrepreneur and believed the Conservative Party were the only political party which could best serve his interests. He encouraged people around him to vote Conservative and constantly went on about how his Caroline Campaigns in 1970 brought Edward Heath to power. 'And look how that turned out,' I repeatedly said. His face would take on an uncomprehending, puzzled expression. I think he really believed Edward Heath was great (simply because he was a Tory). Ronan's attitude towards world events or aspects of his enterprises held many contradictions though. One day, when in response to one of his comments (can't recall what it was) I said, 'steady on Ronan, you're sounding like a socialist there,' he reacted in anger. He claimed to hate socialism. 'Never,' he said, shaking his head. Meaning: he would never be a socialist.

Another day, following a disagreement or clash of politics, when I was thinking he sounded like a right-wing fascist, he turned to me and said 'Well *you*, you're nothing but a brash Aussie sometimes.' He went on to confess that when we'd first met, he'd thought I came from a well-to-do background (like him) in Australia due to the way I spoke and had been disappointed when I'd enlightened him otherwise.

At the time I was confused as to why he'd made the 'brash Aussie' statement out of the blue. Had I verbalised my thoughts about him sounding like a right-wing fascist? Had he read my mind? He appeared to be reacting to me as though I'd said something. I couldn't very well ask him.

He wasn't the only one who believed that I came from a 'posh' background. In the early 70s I was appointed to my job at IPC Magazines because I dressed and spoke well. My boss thought I must have come from a high-ranking Sydney family. I obtained the interview with him because the personnel officer at the employment agency I applied to told him I wasn't a 'normal' Australian. She said this within my hearing (as he'd clearly baulked at the idea of interviewing an Australian). When I challenged her as to what she meant by this comment she said most Australians who came into the Brook St Agency, wore flip flops, t-shirts and shorts (she elaborated by saying they were backpackers) and enunciated words poorly. Being well spoken and wearing smart clothes, she thought I was very different.

I spoke 'well' as Ronan put it because my parents

would not allow me become lazy in my speech and in primary school, we were given elocution lessons, churning out phrases like: 'How now brown cow'. I think my parents' generation and my generation were, by and large, trained to speak with greater clarity (the King's or Queens's English it was often termed) and not allowed to lapse into the use of slang, dropped vowels or consonants. And I don't believe this was restricted to Australia. I found it noticeable in older generations of Londoners when I lived there. I find it noticeable in the older generation of Liverpudlians where I currently live. For the most part, and although they come from a working-class background and all have an identifiable Liverpool accent, it's mild and they speak with eloquence.

Following a disagreement, Ronan and I would uickly move onto other things as though it had never happened. Neither of us ever sulked. He often asked me if I wanted to play backgammon with him following a disagreement. He went through a phase of being addicted to it and some days we would play game after game while work related issues were put aside or forgotten. Even the phone would be ignored – unless Ronan was expecting an important call. We both became experts at it. Whoever went first would always win as we had memorised or worked out every possible move combination. A coin would be tossed to see who went first.

Although large sums of money flowed through Ronan's hands, he never kept a great deal of it for himself. Radio Caroline staff, the film company staff or the band when he was supporting them, were his priority. If Maria was away (and after she moved out) the fridge and larder would often be bare, simply because he had no money.

He played snooker or pool for money and he was pretty damn good at it I was to learn. One evening, after learning that Simon was staying over with a friend, he asked me to accompany him while he played pool.

'I won't eat next week if I don't win some games tonight. You might bring me luck.'

It wasn't how I envisioned spending my free evening but I went along with him out of curiosity. I had no idea that he had to resort to betting on pool games to survive some weeks. Ronan told me it was fairly common for him to do this (and when I mentioned it to Peter Chicago, he confirmed that he knew this to be true). There was no-one at the pub when we first arrived so we played a couple of friendly games together. I was never particularly good at pool unless I had a few drinks under my belt and I wasn't drinking that night as I was driving. Ronan never drank. When the serious players arrived, I stepped back and observed. Ronan bet his last £5 and won. He played more games and won every time. A few hours later he had enough money and withdrew.

Driving home later I thought it seemed rather sad that he had to resort to this to feed himself. But knowing

Ronan as I did, I knew he'd think it preferable to finding traditional employment.

When the Casserole Restaurant across the road from his place became a hang-out joint for him and his mates, Ronan could always rely on one of the businessmen who frequented the place to shout him a meal.

Some weeks he would ask me to meet him at the restaurant rather than in his flat. He took to holding many of his meetings at the Casserole (and using their phone). Well known faces would flit in and out of the place. Marianne Faithful was regularly there when I met up with Ronan – he'd been friends with her since the 60s he told me. I knew she'd starred in *Girl on a Motorcycle* – one of the films he'd made. I became well acquainted with some of his business friends and they constantly asked me to attend one of their parties. Ronan warned me never to go to one (I wasn't interested in doing so anyway). He didn't elaborate regarding party activities but I could well imagine.

Ronan was always paranoid about his phone being bugged by the authorities, so he changed his number with regularity. He was also forced to do this on several occasions as he couldn't afford to pay the bill. Ronan would often spend hours on the phone talking to individuals and ran up enormous bills every quarter. He'd terminate the account and then start another one in a different name. At one point, BT (or whatever it was called back then) would no longer connect a phone to his flat due to a long list of unpaid bills, so Ronan persuaded the person who lived in the basement flat below him to have an extra phone line connected there for him and ran the line upstairs to his place. He couldn't survive without a phone. Apparently, it reached a point where Ronan could no longer access a landline phone in his flat. Peter Chicago related a story about this as follows:

In the last months of the Ross Revenge being at sea it was no longer broadcasting. I left the organisation then but still maintained contact with Ronan. On one of the last occasions when I visited him in London, I first went to his flat but he then took me to a basement room in a side street further down King's Road. The room was very sparsely furnished with a desk and a couple of chairs and most importantly, a telephone. Over the years Ronan had managed to obtain various numbers connected in his flat which were always disconnected because of unpaid bills and at one time he persuaded the occupant of the basement flat to have a second line installed in his flat and then Ronan ran a cable from the basement up to his own flat and used that line until it, too, became disconnected. Having discovered this, BT told Ronan that no further telephone lines would be installed anywhere in Paulton's House (the block Ronan lived in) without checking that extensions or cables were not being diverted into his flat. Hence the need for a separate office with a new phone line down the road.

At the time Ronan was involved in what he called 'The Perfume Project'. He had been told that there was a container load of valuable vintage perfume from one of the major perfumiers in France. It had a total value that could have gone into the millions. Ronan was trying to raise money to buy the consignment of perfume. One of the many complicated deals which he became involved with over the years. Because I lost regular contact with Ronan, I have no idea if that deal proved to be successful.

One day Ronan received a phone call from a man who claimed to be from the Home Office. He told Ronan to call him 'Bob'. He explained that he worked under a Captain Hargreaves in the Marine Offences department. Hargreaves had responsibility for tracking down and arresting anyone who was associated with Radio Caroline.

The department members apparently had to listen to Radio Caroline in shifts around the clock in case someone accidently revealed their real names. They found it no hardship to do this. Ronan's phone and those known to them were also bugged. Namely mine and Oonagh's, Ronan claimed 'Bob' told him. To prove this was true 'Bob' cited details of a phone conversation I'd had with my cousin in Bath. Ronan had no knowledge of my cousin and Oonagh was in France (so she didn't know about my phone conversation and therefore couldn't have mentioned anything to Ronan) so I realised that 'Bob' had to be genuine.

The reason Bob claimed he was contacting Ronan was that Hargreaves was planning to send someone to my flat. Not in a gun blazing style raid – not at that point anyway. He intended a reconnoitre first as though he was on some military expedition (and the title of 'Captain' could have indicated that Hargreaves had a military background). A raid might follow. Bob wanted Ronan to warn me because 'Lyn seems like a nice person and I don't want any difficulties to arise for her or her son Simon,' Ronan claimed 'Bob' told him.

'Bob said you need to get rid of anything you might have at the flat relating to Radio Caroline,' Ronan said.

I did have a load of Caroline stuff in the built-in cupboard in my living room and mentioned this to Ronan.

'Make sure you move out anything linked to Caroline and also anything you have on the film. I don't want them knowing about the film,' he added.

'If they're listening to me as they claim, they'd know about the film work I do. I have to call people.'

'Well get rid of any letter-head you have. Don't forget it has Chris's name on it and they would probably recognise who he is. Bob said that you would never know that anyone had been there looking through your belongings.'

'Okay,' I sighed, a little sceptical about the whole thing. Sure, they might be listening to my phone, but I didn't consider my role as significant enough for the Home Office to be bothered with.

I gathered everything I had into a black bin liner and dropped it into my friend Brenda's place. She wasn't connected to Radio Caroline in any way.

Weeks went by and I saw nothing to indicate that I'd

had a visitor – although I recalled that 'Bob' had said I would never see signs of it. Then one day I returned home to discover I'd had an intruder who had helped themselves to bacon (a whole packet of it – the greedy sod), eggs, toast and tea. They'd left plenty of evidence. A dirty fry pan on top of the cooker; an empty packet of bacon in the bin; the pack of butter left on the countertop; the knife I used for cutting bread sitting on top of the breadboard littered with crumbs from the slices they'd cut; the remainder of the loaf left on the worktop to dry out; a dirty plate, knife, fork, teaspoon and mug in the sink. They'd been rinsed but not washed. The back door was unlocked. I searched the house and found muddy footprints across Simon's bed. Someone had forced open the casement window in his bedroom. They then must have left by the back door and climbed the neighbour's fence. The neighbour to my right, standing in the front of the house, was an end terrace and had a side passage with a gate that was easy enough to traverse.

After checking the flat thoroughly, I realised nothing was missing – except the food. I didn't have any possessions of great value. Nothing looked disturbed or out of place apart from the puzzling mess in the kitchen. Had a hungry burglar broken into my flat? Surely this couldn't be linked to the Home Office 'visit'?

I wasn't sure whether to call the police. I decided it was too insignificant for them to deal with.

When I next saw Ronan, I asked him if he'd heard anything further from his mole Bob. I hadn't mentioned the break-in to him.

I was sceptical about some aspects of the 'Bob' business. If our phones were being tapped then how was Bob able to make his calls without being detected? Surely staff he worked with would recognise his voice?

I'd previously voiced these concerns to Ronan. According to him, Bob was able to make his calls by pausing the tap (*really? – surely that would have to be been done through telephone engineers*). If he was unable to do that, he called another number from a pay phone. A number Ronan had given him. He wouldn't tell me where that other number was located. Apparently 'Bob the mole' would leave a message with the owner of this other phone and say that he'd call back at a particular time. Ronan would need to go to the location to take the call. All very cloak and dagger.

'Everything he says *is* genuine,' Ronan insisted. 'He calls me Bob also. Bob Kennedy.'

Bob Kennedy was one of Ronan's pseudonyms.

'Yes he's called,' Ronan said in response to my question. 'He said to tell you your visitor enjoyed the meal and they didn't find anything so there will be no raid. What's with the meal business?'

I told him then what had happened and he laughed.

'It's not funny,' I retorted. 'I've got to pay to have the window fixed – and buy a new pack of bacon!'

'At least your flat won't be raided,' he added.

There was that.

8

I took a few weeks off all my jobs in August 1976. Simon and I joined up with a group of people and spent three weeks camping on a beach in Santorini, one of the Greek Islands. I wanted some hot sun, sand and sea to remind me of Australia. The volcanic sand in Santorini was nothing like Australian beaches but it was largely an enjoyable experience. I returned to England to discover temperatures in the UK had exceeded those we'd encountered in Santorini.

The year plodded on with my various jobs, college and home life. James, the presenter I went to Sheffield with back in '75, started calling around to my place regularly when he was on shore leave. An attraction developed but we were both reticent about taking it further. He was younger than me and I had never been involved with a younger man. The long hair of the Sheffield trip that hid his face was long gone and I thought he was a very good-looking young man.

According to my passport the first trip I'd made to Boulogne was in October 1975. I didn't travel there again until June 1976 (unless my passport wasn't stamped). Back then we stayed at the Alexander Hotel near the port. On that June 76 trip I complained to Oonagh about the lousy restaurants around Boulogne which seemed to be catering to English tourists. We decided to scour the back streets to see if we could find an authentic French restaurant. We found one in a quiet lane and had a fabulous (and much cheaper) meal. No-one in the restaurant spoke English and a mixed group at another table encouraged us to join them at a 'secret' French only nightclub. Oonagh and I joined them where we danced and chatted until the early hours of the following morning. Again no one spoke English in this club so I was forced to churn out my schoolgirl French. We ate at the same restaurant several more times on my subsequent visits but I never returned to the nightclub.

By December 1976 Oonagh had acquired residency status in France and rented a flat. Instead of expensive hotel bills, the changeover staff for Caroline could now crash at the flat the night before departure and those returning could stay overnight on their return. I didn't deal with the finances for the flat so I don't know how economical it was to have a permanent flat to rent against the cost of hotel bills. The location of the flat was to prove disastrous for Radio Caroline in the long term though.

Shortly before James went out to the boat in December '76 we became involved. We kept it quiet though as we didn't know where it was going. Oonagh however caught us embracing over in France and wasn't pleased.

I don't know why. She had a boyfriend in Boulogne and it wasn't as though she was interested in James. However, there'd been an incident earlier in the year that led to Oonagh being sharp towards him and he was convinced she didn't like him. He avoided her as much as he could. He was quite a shy young man, lacking in confidence until he felt comfortable with you and he'd always preferred collecting his pay from me as we'd become acquainted on the Sheffield trip.

From that trip on I started receiving regular letters from 'James.' He has kindly given permission for me to paraphrase or include quotes from them.

The first letter I received was in January 1977, followed by another dated 2nd February 1977.

There was a belief among the staff that DJ Tony Allen was ripping off supplies that were intended for the boat (Tony had a reputation for this). James says:

'It's not Tony Allen ripping off supplies.'

James had apparently been looking for a carrier bag back in the flat and came across 'loads of stuff' he believed Oonagh's man was putting aside for himself.

'Only 75% of the produce purchased was delivered to the boat,' he says.

James had been on the shopping trip where all the goods had been purchased and made a mental note of it all.

The disappearance of goods could have been down to the tender crew. It is unlikely however. Back in those days the young men who ran the tenders were very decent. They were paid handsomely for the work and had no real reason to steal supplies to increase their profit. Later tender crew, who weren't paid so well, might think differently.

Also, in the 2nd February letter James says:

'There's no water. We're only allowed to brush our teeth with Vittel 1 or 2 a day.'

'There's been no water for showers for 2 weeks.'

He kept himself busy working on the record library to avoid certain people. Johnny Jason was complaining all the time about music and the situation. One of the engineers they called 'Napoleon' and another called the 'mechanic' were also being a pain. Napoleon, so named by the DJs for his stature and dictatorial ways (and resemblance to Bonaparte) was a transmitter engineer and one of the few who had worked on Caroline in the 60s.

James attempted to cheer everyone up by making tea. He used a can of water that was in the kitchen believing it had been put aside for use there. It turned out that it was reject water with diesel oil in it. He spent 45 minutes cleaning the kettle after and was not popular.

Later he goes on to say:

'There's no bread, no water, no milk, 1 generator, little food, and low morale.'

They saw a light on the horizon and became excited thinking it might be a tender but it came no closer. The tender (a Dutch one) finally arrived the next day and his letters were sent off with them.

The next letter is dated 10/2/77.

James says: 'I received a four-sided letter from 'O''

'O' said he'd made a load of noise in the flat on the Sunday before departure. The letter was all about 'How to use the apartment properly'.

I don't recall the intricate details of the flat with so much distance in time. I remember it was large and comfortable. However, Peter Chicago, Caroline's long-serving engineer, said the pipes in the flat used to make a hell of a racket when they showered or washed. They'd often arrive late at night, filthy dirty after not being able to shower on board or wash their clothes if there were water shortages (and there often was) so one by one they'd jump in the shower, and be using it until the early hours of the morning. Peter used to keep himself clean on the ship by using a combination of warm sea water and either washing up liquid or shampoo which would lather up well and not leave his skin dry. He said most of the DJ's were young though and had little experience of living away from home so their personal hygiene deteriorated over the weeks (they wouldn't use sea water for washing – although their clothes were washed in twin tubs using sea water).

After having a booze up at the flat in celebration of their return to dry land, they would dispose of bottles down the rubbish shoot on the landing. It made a loud echoing noise. Neighbours apparently complained about all the noise. With hindsight, renting the apartment was not a wise move.

There used to be regular aeroplane drops from the

Netherlands which contained pre-recorded programmes for the Dutch station. The drops would also include treats for the staff. They would need to take the rubber dinghy out to collect the drop but in his letter of 10/2/77 James says:

'The Irish Engineer refused to go out and Tony wouldn't get up.'

Tony was another transmitter engineer.

Other snippets from that letter include:

'Stuart was sick all day.

'The generators stopped. Sirens were going off. The fan belt was not put on properly and both stations were off the air for 25 minutes.'

'We were off air again overnight.'

'The Dutch are peeved they're not in control at present.'

James went on to say that when the Dutch organised things, they had good food, plus plenty of water and oil supplies.

In his letter dated 17th to 18th February 77 James says: 'The engineer walked off in a fit of rage.' He doesn't specify which engineer or where he walked off to. There were different types of engineers on board the ship. I had visions of him walking off the side of the boat into the sea.

He goes on to say: 'Generators are not working properly. There is air getting into the fuel causing it to stop.'

'We were plunged into darkness so we made tea.' (the cooker was run by a gas cylinder)

A tender finally arrived and 'Stuart and Mike left'. He doesn't say who, if anyone, took their place.

They sent the rubber dinghy out for the aeroplane drop but it didn't come. The seas turned really rough and 'everything was flying about', James says.

They cleaned the bilges out but water was coming in. They heard that the Mebo II was anchored off the Dutch Coast playing Radio Northsea's theme tune every 5 minutes and believed they were soon going to have competition.

He later says:

'I had my first wash for 10 days this morning. It was heaven. I used three saucepans. 1 hot, 1 cold and 1 for rinsing.'

Unfortunately for James, the rinsing one hadn't been washed properly and had the remnants of chicken soup in it. He claimed he went around with his hair smelling of chicken soup for days after.

There's a gap in the letter then James says he had to stop writing at that point because a large wave hit the ship covering it with water 'which was coming in everywhere.'

The next day the cook Paul (who James says is a good cook) went on strike because of the mess everywhere. To placate him James cleaned up the kitchen and made a meal for three of them. Beans, sausages, chips and eggs.

They repaired the hatch in the studio so water couldn't come in.

They had an aeroplane drop from the Dutch side that day which included a message saying: 'Oonagh has left the organisation and Jane has taken over.'

None of us had ever heard of Jane. She may have been someone that the Dutch employed to organise things on their side. They may have asked Ronan to get rid of Oonagh and let them put this Jane in her place. He might have gone along with it to keep them happy for the time being. If that was the case, he never said a word about it. Oonagh had not left the 'organisation' (as yet) and we never saw or met a woman called Jane. She remained a mystery.

We had to organise tenders for the exchange of Caroline presenters because Ronan told us that the managers of the Dutch radio station, Mi Amigo (which also broadcasted from the ship) would only take the engineers (who were vital for the Dutch as well) on their tenders. This wasn't entirely true as English presenters occasionally travelled out or back with Dutch personnel. I can imagine it's what the Dutch Bosses wanted though. They were already paying Ronan quite a lot of money.

The last time I drove across to Boulogne with records for Radio Caroline was on New Year's Eve in December 1976 when I travelled with James. From then on, I was no longer able to do my usual run collecting new releases. I can't remember the precise details but my recollection is that EMI, were approached by the British Government requesting that they cease providing us with music. Seen by many as the leader in the industry, EMI wrote to all the other companies asking them to stop providing us with records. One by one, the companies pulled out, telling me they'd received this letter from EMI.

When some mention was made over the air that

companies were no longer supplying records to Caroline, a Caroline fan, who owned a record store somewhere along either the Suffolk or Essex coast, volunteered to provide them. Thereafter, all the albums came from him. I don't know how they were transported to the boat, but I no longer had to do the Boulogne runs with them.

It was on my return trip from Boulogne on 1st January 1977 that I was finally challenged as to why I made so many short trips to Europe. The custom official had scoured through my passport checking dates. I was held at Dover for hours while they stripped the car out, checking it for 'drugs or weapons' they claimed. I assume they thought I might have weapons because I had an Irish passport and might be linked to the IRA. Of course, they found nothing – it was on the way over there was something to find (the records). When the customs official challenged me, I trotted out the cover story of the wealthy boyfriend. I wasn't asked to name the 'boyfriend' or provide details of where we'd met. The customs official sniggered and sneered, mumbling and laughing with his peers (who were searching my car) about it. It didn't faze me. I just stood waiting patiently for them to complete their search. After the car seats and door upholstery were reassembled, I was cleared to leave.

I believe it was on my next trip to Boulogne, at the end of January 77, that I delivered a left-hand drive silver Ford Fiesta to Oonagh and I would have returned to the UK by ferry and train. I can't recall whether Oonagh bought the car in the UK, or had driven over to England with it and then returned to France by other means.

It's at this point that the time line becomes fuzzy and confusing for me. It was my belief that things didn't get out of control until later that year. When everything started going wrong Ronan sent me to Boulogne to see what was going on. I would travel either from Folkestone direct to Boulogne or from Dover to Calais and then drive down. At Dover, Customs always stamped my passport. At Folkestone, they didn't always do so. Similarly, custom officials at Heathrow Airport always stamped my passport; they didn't always do so at Gatwick. So, because I have no stamps from Dover or Folkestone after March '77, I don't know if it's because I travelled via Folkestone and received no stamp or whether I ceased to go there and events happened much earlier than I believed. I only know that matters got seriously out of hand and everything was dumped on me to deal with. My last stamp for a French trip was on 20-21 March 1977. It was either on that trip or a later one from Boulogne that I was questioned again about my brief trips to Europe on re-entry to England. I was a foot passenger on the ferry on that particular trip but once again was subjected to the sneers and sniggers of the British Customs officials (who always seemed to be men) when I mentioned the 'wealthy boyfriend'.

9

Sometime in 1977, Oonagh hired a young Dutch student called Joanna (not her real name) as a cleaner for her flat. She was 20 years old, in her final year at university and spoke English with an American accent. Joanna was a shapely, attractive young woman, with long hair pulled off her face into a ponytail.

A little at a time, Oonagh drew Joanna into doing things for Caroline.

'You barely know her,' I pointed out to Oonagh. 'How do you know she can be trusted?'

'She'll be fine,' was Oonagh's response. Famous last words.

University courses traditionally finished by the early summer in June. I either wasn't aware of it, or forgot, but apparently Joanna did a stint on the boat that summer as a cook. Oonagh would have sent her out there.

Perhaps Oonagh advised her to cut her hair off for ease of care on the ship, but according to Peter Chicago Joanna had short hair when she went onboard. He has a distinct memory of Joanna scuttling up the mast for him one day in an attempt to repair it.

Females on the boat were rare in the 70s. Peter Chicago's long-standing girlfriend Ellen was an exception. She presented shows under the name of Samantha. When I was told Ellen was due to be on board, I hired a friend, Annie (not her real name) to go out there as the cook.

Annie did a couple of stints on the boat. She was a friend of mine and Brenda's who we had known for some years. Shortly before I hired her, she'd been involved in the running of a restaurant down in South Norwood, but wanted to get away from the crazy lifestyle she'd been leading there (lots of sex and booze). When Brenda, the kids (Claudia and Simon) and I visited Annie at the restaurant one evening, I was shocked to discover that a man called Peter was one of the regulars who hung out there and who Annie had sex with. I had worked as a 'temp' with this man for a few weeks in a London office in 1972 around the time I first moved into my flat at Oonagh's property. He must have followed me home one day and discovered where I lived. When I first spotted him outside my place, I asked what he was doing there. He said he wanted to 'be with me'. I told him I wasn't interested but he continued to turn up. He started stalking me and would stand outside my 'flat' for hours on end, never attempting to approach me, just standing out there. It was very strange and rather creepy. It wasn't until Sonny saw him off with some harsh words that he finally gave up.

When Annie said she wanted to 'get away' from the

crazy life, I was happy to oblige. I didn't think it healthy for her to be around that man. I was no doubt prejudiced from my experiences of him, but Annie said Peter was a 'little strange'. I didn't need further convincing, so when we needed a cook, I hired Annie – on the promise that she wouldn't attempt to get every single man on board into her bed (particularly James). Annie loved sex but claimed she was a little fed up with it. She promised she'd restrict her sexual encounters to a few men. I was worried though and envisioned conflict arising among the males on board. However, it seemed to go okay.

I received a short letter from Annie from the Netherlands in April '77. She might have been staying in the Netherlands with Ellen. The two women became friends and had either at this point left the ship for good or were due to go out again later that year.

In late June 1977 James, Simon and I travelled to Ireland for several weeks. It was a holiday I'd been planning for some time. I waited until I'd received results of my final exams at college before setting off (I passed). I was due to travel with my cousin from Bath to Wexford, where he had a cottage. The cottage was one that my mother and my cousin's mother (my great Aunt Eve) had inherited.

My mother's understanding of the inheritance was that she had jointly inherited land with her aunt (Eve). On my brother's marriage, he had been the recipient of money from the sale of my grandmother's house in Sydney (which he wisely put into his own house).

Foolishly, my mother lent much of the remaining money to a friend who lost it all in a failed business venture and never repaid her. I therefore didn't receive a penny. My mother said, when the money from the Irish inheritance came through, I was to have it all. I was excited at the prospect and planned to invest in a block of land in a Sydney beach suburb. Something that I'd been wanting to do for a couple of years.

Aunt Eve told my mother that a farmer had been leasing the land, it was pretty worthless and they supposedly ended up out of pocket with solicitor's costs. In other words, my mother and hence me, didn't receive a penny. The whole thing really upset my mother and she kept apologising over it. At the time she showed me all the correspondence and the solicitor's bill concerning it.

The Wexford cottage came up in conversation with my cousin J____ during one of my visits to him in Bath. He told me that he had owned it jointly with his mother, but on her recent death, he owned it outright.

'Of course, it was the cottage that mother and your mother inherited,' he told me. 'I bought out your mother's share.'

This was news to me and I related the story that his mother had told my mother.

'My mother showed me the solicitor's bill,' I told him. 'She had to send money to *your* mother for her share of the bill – minus the pittance they received for the land.'

'They didn't sell the land,' he insisted. 'They *exchanged* the land, which was far more valuable to the farmer, for a cottage and a few acres he owned. I bought your mother out.'

'Well, your mother didn't mention any cottage, nor did my mother receive any money for it,' I told him.

J____ wouldn't believe me, nor could he accept that his mother would do anything like that. Since her death, she'd become a saint. Prior to that, he'd complained about her all the time. I'd already related to him the story of the antiques. In the 60s, after having a number of antiques valued, his mother Eve conned my mother into sending them over to her in Ireland. Eve claimed she wanted to buy these antiques following my grandmother's death. However, Eve never paid my mother the money she owed for them, insisting that as they had belonged to her sister, she was entitled to them. They weren't left to Eve though and they weren't *family* heirlooms handed down from the sisters' parents. My grandmother collected antiques and these were items she'd bought after moving to Australia. Eve had coveted them since seeing them on a visit to Sydney. They were so valuable, J____ had, since his inheritance, locked the same antiques in a bank vault. He *knew* his mother had acquired her assets partially through devious means. She'd done it much of her life in order to survive since she'd found herself a young, spurned (by her first husband), pregnant (with J____'s much older brother) woman who was alone in a tough man's world in the late 1920s. It didn't make it right though.

Anyway, Jonathon made a big deal that year about me, Simon and James, joining him at the cottage. He'd invited various friends over there at different times – but never me. We were due to stay there for a few days before going our separate ways. I was looking for a gay friend of mine from Sydney, Don, who'd moved back home to somewhere in County Cork. J____ was also planning to track down an old childhood friend.

I rang J____ at home a couple of days before we were due to leave to make final arrangements, only to be told by his boyfriend, R___, that he'd already left. He was surprised that I didn't know he'd gone, or have details of where the property was. R___ claimed not to know the address of the property as he'd never been there. He was a teacher and schools hadn't broken up yet so he couldn't accompany J____, who always went over to Ireland during term time.

So, at the last moment we had to book into a hotel in Wexford. We stayed there for a few days before heading down to Cork City where I had the address of a relative of Don's. I knew that Don was managing a hotel he owned somewhere in Cork County. It had always been his dream to manage, and one day own his own hotel. He had finally achieved it. Don had persuaded me to go to Jersey in the Channel Islands where his brother lived and asked me if I would go into hotel management with him there. I went on ahead and he was due to follow. He didn't end up coming to Jersey after all, and a few years later returned to Ireland instead.

Don's family gave me the address and his phone number. I phoned Don and he was overjoyed to hear from me. He invited us to come and stay at the hotel. The hotel was in a village near Mallow, on the Blackwater River.

Don's partner (both in business and life) was called Ian. Ian had invested money into the hotel but didn't work there. He worked for the forestry commission during the day and spent most evenings propping up the bar, making scathing comments about the restaurant and bar customers, who, apart from some hotel residents, were made up largely of people from the local village.

We quickly came to realise that Ian had grown up with my cousin J____ and another friend called John F, who also lived in London and who I met up with regularly. I suspected that Ian was the childhood friend that J____ was searching for. It was a small world. A few days before leaving the hotel I rang Bath and spoke to R___. He confirmed that the friend J____ was trying to locate was called Ian and J___ was returning home as he'd had no success. I promptly bought a postcard from Mallow and sent it to him, with 'Wish you were here', pointing out that his friend Ian, was with my friend Don. I also said it was a *shame* he hadn't been able to trace him.

I could see that Don was on the point of collapse through exhaustion. He worked very long hours in the hotel and hadn't had a break since taking it over. After discussing it with James, I suggested that Don and Ian take a few days off and I would run things in his absence. My other reason for suggesting it was that I could see that tension was building with customers from Ian's hostile and drunken behaviour. The two men jumped at the chance and disappeared.

With me running the hotel, it meant that I couldn't give James or Simon a great deal of attention. Simon was always an easy-going, adaptable child though and I knew he would be fine hanging around me while I worked. As long as he had a comic, or a book. He was always happy to help and made himself useful, fetching me things in the kitchen (like different vegetables). He was almost 6 years old by then. I would take an afternoon break and was able to spend quality time with him then.

That hotel was one of the strangest places I have ever worked. It was quite surreal and a place of role reversal which made me smile. In the kitchen and behind the scenes in other jobs, impoverished landed gentry worked. All protestant with posh 'English' accents. The main customers of the restaurant and bar were who Ian scornfully called 'the catholic peasants' (Ian was an Irish protestant who also spoke with an English accent) were residents of the local village and their families would have once worked the land for the lord of the manor (the hotel would have been the manor house back in the day).

Whilst there, Don took me to a few of the large properties where members of his staff lived. They owned huge acreage with crumbling mansions and were regular participators in 'fox hunts' with hounds. Don didn't take part in the hunts, but Ian did.

When they returned from their short break, Don and Ian attempted to persuade me to move in permanently with them and open a 'protestant' school on the land. There were a number of outbuildings that could be converted with the aid of grants from the Irish government, they said. Apparently, attracted to Ireland due to available farming grants, a number of Dutch and German families had moved into the region. They didn't want their children to attend local Catholic schools so either home schooled them or sent them away to boarding school. They hated doing this and would have preferred to have their children at home with them. Ian claimed to have spoken to a number of the families, who all said they'd love it if a school on their grounds was available.

'I've only just qualified as a teacher,' I reminded them. 'And, apart from my teaching practises, I've barely taught, and have no experience of running a school.'

'Oh, you'd be fine,' Don said dismissively.

They also came up with the brilliant idea of having children with me.

'You can marry Don, have his child. Then divorce him, marry me and have my child,' Ian said. 'We both want children.'

The idea of having a child to each of the gay men did not appeal to me. Were they considering artificial insemination? I didn't want to know. I politely declined both the school and the marriage proposals.

It's a good thing that I didn't take them up on the offer of opening a school. They were forced to sell the hotel and move the following year. When I met up with Don and Ian in London some years later, Don revealed the real reason they'd sold. Apparently, Ian's verbal abuse and hostility towards the locals reached fever pitch. They started receiving serious anonymous warnings that they couldn't ignore.

My cousin J____ had also apparently caused minor conflict amongst his neighbours around the cottage in Wexford. The cottage sat on land with planning permission to build several more houses. It mysteriously burnt down and the insurers wouldn't compensate J____ as it had been left unoccupied for longer than the policy allowed. Planning permission had expired and the local council would not renew it. J____ was forced to sell the land at a much-reduced value than it had previously held. Karma.

As for the priceless antiques his mother had swindled my mother over. Fed up with paying charges for the bank vault, J____ put them on display in his house where his many visitors could see them (he ran a business from his home). In the 80s while on a holiday with John F in the Canary Islands during either January or February, his house was broken into and they were all stolen. His insurance didn't cover the antiques as he'd never declared them. J____ was convinced that John F and I were the masterminds behind the burglary. He believed John F had lured him away from his house on the pretext of a holiday (even though they went to the Canaries most years around this time) and that I went to the property and removed all the items. He relayed his theories to the police (and both John F and me) but neither of us heard from the police so I don't think they took him seriously. More Karma.

James, understandably, was not pleased by Don and Ian's proposals; they had not included him in any of their suggestions. He became hostile towards the pair.

James had been neglected while I ran the hotel. After working long hours each day, Simon was my priority. He also, no doubt, felt left out when Don and I reminisced about our life in Sydney. He became moody and uncommunicative. I felt for him.

At the end of the holiday, it was apparent our relationship was not working though. We called it quits.

10

When Oonagh enquired how the holiday in Ireland had gone I told her James and I had parted ways. At no point did I say that I was feeling bereft by the split. I kept details of the holiday to a minimum – although I had told her that I'd relieved Don for a few days. She must have then passed the information on to Ronan. When I next saw him, Ronan was wearing his sympathetic face.

'I'm sorry to hear about your break-up,' he said. 'I've been talking to George and he has offered the use of his home to you and Simon.'

'George?' I asked, wondering who on earth he was talking about.

'George Harrison. He said you and Simon are welcome to stay at Friar Park and you could have your own independent accommodation there if you didn't want to mix with him or his friends. Did you know he and Pattie have split up? He's not always there as he travels a lot – but he's there at the moment.'

The Patti Ronan was referring to, was Patti Boyd, George's ex-wife. I was aware of their split. It had been splattered across newspapers.

I knew Ronan was friends with George Harrison – since I'd known him, he'd mentioned George a number of times. When he'd first said 'George' though I simply didn't make the connection. Why on earth would I? I didn't know him.

'That's very kind of George,' I said. And I did think it was a kind offer but I wondered what had prompted him to make it. 'But are you trying to match-make me with George, Ronan?' I asked him. 'If so, it's a crazy idea.'

'No, No,' he said. 'I just thought when George offered his place to you, it might be a quiet space for you to get over your break-up.'

'I'm fine, Ronan,' I said.

'Well why don't you go to Henley anyway and just take a bit of time to relax away from everything. From what Oonagh told me you were working while you were in Ireland.'

'Yes, but I only worked for a few days. What's going on Ronan?' I asked him.

'Nothing,' he insisted now wearing his innocent looking face. 'I just thought a break might be good for you. And George's home is a wonderful place to take a break.'

'Well, thank you, but I don't need it.'

I suspected there was an agenda underlying Ronan's suggestion. I believed he may well have exaggerated my situation, manipulating George into making the offer. Ronan had an agenda behind most things he did.

I had discovered Ronan's agenda for insisting that my name be listed on the film company's letterhead as L. Gilbert and signing all correspondence as L. Gilbert, was so that people in the business might mistakenly believe the letter was from Lewis Gilbert, a well-known British film director and producer.

At Elvaston Place one Friday afternoon, I commented on how quickly companies responded to my letters. It was either Tim or Dick who said, 'That's because they think you're Lewis Gilbert.'

I'd never heard of Lewis Gilbert, but when they enlightened me on his films, I'd certainly heard of, or seen most of them. It's strange that Lewis Gilbert's name hadn't entered my consciousness. I would have thought having the same surname as me, I would have found it noticeable. I knew the names of other directors, such as David Lean, John Huston, John Ford to name but a few. But somehow, Lewis Gilbert's name had completely passed me by.

'Ah, so that's why Ronan wanted me to work for him then,' I replied, a little disappointed that he hadn't considered I might be an asset due to my potential capabilities. It was simply because of my name.

After learning about Lewis Gilbert, I challenged Ronan over it. He grinned at me but denied that was why he'd wanted me to list my name as L. Gilbert or sign everything that way. He hadn't wanted me to use the initial of my middle name either. I usually signed everything as L.P. Gilbert.

He insisted that he believed companies would

respond more to me if they *thought* I was a man, reminding me that we lived in chauvinistic society. He said that it was common for men to use their initials on company letterhead and hadn't wanted anything that might indicate I was a woman.

'I'm sure that was part of your thinking Ronan, but that doesn't explain why I couldn't include the 'P'.'

'It kept things simple. In case anything was to go wrong. Gilbert is not an unusual name.'

I think I understood what he meant then. Ronan was a person who was used to ducking and diving to avoid paying bills and used a range of pseudonyms throughout his working life. If we'd included the 'P' then it would narrow down the number of people with the same initials if I needed to be traced. My home address was not registered on any documents linked to the company. Our registered address by this time was with our auditors in London, N3. I had correspondence sent to Elvaston Place.

Using just the 'L' would increase the number of people it could be in the British population. Although not a very common name, there are, nevertheless, quite a few Gilberts in the country.

I wasn't concerned about anything 'going wrong'. I had control of the purse strings. I didn't run up debts I couldn't cover. But I forgot that I was dealing with Ronan O'Rahilly. I was soon to learn.

Now I wondered what the agenda was with George, as there was bound to be one. I wasn't to discover what that was until the following year.

11

It was routine to broadcast a set of numbers at 9pm each night so that those of us back on dry land knew how things were going out at sea. The numbers ranged from 1 to 30 back in those days. If high numbers were broadcast there were serious problems. High numbers started to be broadcast most nights. I think this was in the autumn of 1977 but as previously mentioned, I might have that wrong. The events that followed aren't though.

James was out on the ship, as was Stuart Russell, Roger Matthews, Ellen and Annie. I don't know who else.

Shortly before he'd travelled out to the ship James had come to see me. He'd learned from other Caroline presenters that I had a broken foot, which had happened from jumping over a tiny creek on Hampstead Heath in late August. I'd landed badly on the foot; it had twisted under me and snapped the bones and torn the ligaments. I had broken the same foot several times in the past. He was worried as to how I was managing financially.

Actually, I was doing very well. The company I worked for who made toiletry bags had put a proposition to me after my injury. I was unable to drive into work, so the boss proposed that he would have someone pick me up each morning, drop Simon to school (schools resumed shortly after my accident), I'd work all day without a break then in the afternoon a member of staff would drive me to Simon's school to collect him and drop us home. He even agreed to have me chauffeured to a supermarket once a week so that I could be assisted with shopping. He was offering me a very generous salary, plus a monthly bonus.

His company had dramatically expanded since I'd first started doing his accounts and he wanted me there all the time. He knew though, that as newly qualified teacher, I was likely to be applying for a job in a school. I hadn't applied for any teaching jobs before leaving college as we were told it was a hopeless situation. For every teaching vacancy (apart from Science and Maths) more than 200 people applied. The UK Government had done its usual thing of cutting teacher training places and creating a shortage of teachers to fill the jobs early in the 70s (they did the same with nurses). So, they'd imported teachers (and nurses) from overseas, largely from Commonwealth countries, and by June 77, when I finished college, there were too many teachers.

The one stipulation my boss made with the proposal was that I had to commit to working for him for a full year, by which time he would find other people to replace me if I wanted to leave. It was an offer I couldn't refuse.

I couldn't get out and about easily with my broken foot, so it was great to have visitors. James came to see me several times and shortly before he left to go back out to the ship, we agreed that we'd give our relationship another go. Letters started arriving from him once again. I was to receive two that made it off the ship. But before I received them, an alert had been raised indicating conditions on the ship were deteriorating from the high numbers being broadcast.

I don't recall what each number stood for, but the numbers being read out meant they were running out of food, water and oil.

Phone calls to Oonagh, who was at the flat in Boulogne, provided no answers. She insisted all was well. Tenders had been sent out by her regularly with plenty of provisions but it wasn't possible to have a changeover of staff just yet. No explanation was given as to why and it wasn't something that we could go into detail on in phone calls. What was missing though was the larger tenders with bulk supplies of food, water and oil. She had been told that the larger tenders had been delayed due to poor weather.

Ronan told most people that the large tender ships came from Spain – a country where it was legal to provide supplies to Caroline as they weren't part of the European Union, nor had they ratified the Marine offences Act that Britain introduced (whereas France, Belgium and the Netherlands had). Spain hadn't been able to apply to join the European Union until after

Franco's death when they became a democracy. The membership process took some time and they didn't actually join until the mid-80s. However, the truth was, bulk supply ships mainly came from either the Netherlands or Belgium where it was illegal. Neither Oonagh or I were ever involved in organising these supplies. The Dutch radio organisation which operated from the Mi Amigo, had this responsibility.

After repeatedly hearing the high numbers, Ronan phoned me asking me to call over to his flat. If this was in the autumn my foot was out of plaster by then and I was able to drive again. It might have been back in March however. When I arrived, he gave me the name and phone number of a man who lived near Peckham in south London.

'You need to make contact with John, he'll be able to do ship to shore and get to the bottom of what the problem is.'

I knew there were occasional ship to shore contacts made, but had never been given any details. Ronan liked to keep people in compartments – never meeting.

John (perhaps not his real name) seemed concerned but cagey when I made the call. He agreed to meet up. I had someone else connected to Caroline travel down there with me. Once again with the passage of time, I can't recall who accompanied me but I know I was uncomfortable about visiting the home of a man I didn't know on my own. Simon was also with me, as we made the trip on a Saturday.

John had a house full of people present when we

arrived. I believe John, and those in the house with him were what the DJ's called anoraks – fans of Radio Caroline.

He explained how difficult it was to achieve the ship to shore. It wasn't always possible to reach them if no one was in the vicinity of the radio – they didn't always have it switched on. They had to use different locations every time they did it and as soon as they made the connection, they could be tracked and attempts would be made to catch them. He had the relevant equipment though and was willing to keep trying with his mate until he got through. He said he'd be in touch.

John did manage to get through to them at some point the following week. After receiving a call from him I headed off to see him to discover what he'd learned. It wasn't safe to exchange information over the phone.

Things were dire on the ship as the numbers predicted. They weren't receiving food and drink supplies and oil and water supplies were very low.

In his letter dated 26th September 77 (not received until November) James says very little about it – only that they had 'no food, no water and no milk'.

In his letter dated November 77, things are sounding more desperate.

'We're down to beans and rice every day plus we have a couple of packets of dried soup left.'

'There's no electricity during the day – generators are turned off from dawn to dusk.'

This was due to the shortage of oil.

'We cannot check our position with radar or make contact

with anyone.'

Things were sounding dreadful. I received the letters in November when they were taken off by a Dutch tender.

Before some brief respite arrived from the Dutch tender, Ronan sent me over to France with a fistful of money to make sure some emergency supplies reached the boat. He said he shouldn't need to give me money as Ernst was sending money through to Oonagh all the time. But he gave it to me in case there'd been a problem.

I remember that I travelled by train and ferry.

In France Oonagh explained that she'd had to change tender providers. She said the ones we'd always used (who were completely trustworthy and reliable) would no longer make the trips and that they were too expensive anyway.

According to Offshore Echoes, our regular tender providers had been arrested in January that year. I can't be sure but I don't think that prevented them from making further trips out. I think they experienced another incident that prevented them from carrying on.

The same Offshore Echoes site mentions Oonagh as being arrested in March the same year along with other owners of fishing vessels. Oonagh was to appear in court in June 77. Was this when matters blew up in Boulogne or was it an earlier arrest? It was common for Caroline employees to be arrested over the years but it never deterred them from returning. Oonagh told me that following the arrest that ended everything for us in Boulogne she was kept in jail and when released, kicked out of Boulogne and told *never to return*. If that was the case, why would she be asked to return in June for a court appearance?

The problem with this time line is that no-one can remember when it all happened in 1977. I have used clues from James's letters. I knew Annie was the cook on that fateful trip. In his letters during the Spring, he refers to a cook called Paul.

Back in Boulogne I asked Oonagh who she was currently using to take supplies out to the ship.

'A French fisherman,' she told me. 'He won't change the crews though. Yet. But I might be able to persuade him to.'

'Well supplies are not reaching the boat,' I told her. 'They have no food or drinking water.'

'That's not true. I sent a boat out just last week full of supplies.'

'Well they haven't stopped broadcasting high numbers that indicate otherwise. Perhaps the fisherman is not actually making the trip. Just keeping the money and all the supplies.'

'I don't believe he'd not make the trip.' But she conceded he might be ripping off supplies. 'I'll see if we can find someone else,' she said. 'I'm sure I can get it cheaper anyway.'

Oonagh finding someone else necessitated us taking a trip that evening to some dodgy bars down near the dock. The hairs stood up on the back of my neck when we walked into one bar. The male characters in there (and I can't remember there being any females) looked like the rough, stereotypical images you'd see in films set anywhere in the world – of dangerous men; men you would cross at your peril. From the scowling looks they gave us we weren't welcome in there.

Oonagh was unperturbed though and leaving me at a table on my own, approached a group of men. After some discussion and handshaking, she returned.

'He's a fisherman and is willing to go out very early tomorrow. We have to go shopping first and deliver the supplies down to him.' She beamed with pride when she told me she got him for less money than the last one she'd used.

'Is the last one you used in this bar?' I asked her.

'No, he was in the bar we've just left.'

'And he knew you were in there looking for someone else?'

She shrugged.

I thought she was playing a dangerous game. They didn't seem like the type of men you either double-crossed or made deals with others behind their back.

'Are you sure what you're doing is safe Oonagh?' I asked her, concerned.

'Yes,' she said nodding. We left the bar at my urging; it wasn't a place I wanted to hang around and I think we went shopping straight away – to a 24-hr hypermarket. I'd been to the hypermarket with Oonagh a few times in the past. They sold quality kids clothes at a low price. I'd bought Simon loads of 'French' t-shirts there (and cheap red wine if I was driving back).

At the hypermarket we bought loads of bottled water,

meat, fresh vegetables, tin vegetables and fruit, dried goods, chocolates, plus wine and beer. The bill came to about £250 which went a long way back then. The supplies were only meant to last them a few weeks until the large tender could make it out. I can't remember if we also bought cigarettes separately. We probably did. Apparently, cigarettes and tobacco were a standard item supplied to the ship.

We delivered the goods to the dock in Oonagh's car and unloaded it in the dark. The fishermen who loaded it onto the boat didn't speak to us. I wondered if it would all arrive at the ship.

When James finally came off, I discovered that the fisherman did go out that day. Only a fraction of the shopping was delivered though and those on board couldn't understand why we would send a boat all the way from France with so little. We didn't. The French fishermen were clearly stealing the supplies which they no doubt justified by thinking Oonagh was paying them far too little for the trip.

Before leaving Boulogne, I visited our previous suppliers, to see if I could convince them to start going out again.

'It's too risky,' they said and wouldn't agree to it.

On a previous trip I'd made to Boulogne, Oonagh had gone out to dinner with a Chief Police Inspector. He was quite a bit older than Oonagh if I remember him correctly. I only saw him briefly. According to Nigel Harris's book *Ships in Troubled Waters*, the Inspector lived in the same block of flats which was no doubt how they met. I can no longer recall the details. The police in Boulogne knew that we were operating out of their town. It was illegal, but they'd always turned a blind eye.

I queried with Oonagh whether it was wise to have any association with the Inspector, but she assured me her 'friendship' with him would keep him on our side. Sadly, that wasn't how things worked out.

12

One night there was a knock at my door and when I opened it, I discovered Ellen and Annie standing there. I knew they were supposed to be on the ship and wondered how on earth they'd made it back to the UK when as far as I knew no further tenders who would change staff had gone out. Perhaps the bulk supply ship had been out. But I soon learned otherwise.

'We jumped ship, so we could come back and tell you how bad everything is. Only the Belgium sailors who took us off made us sail around with them for three weeks first. Otherwise we would have been here sooner.'

They went into detail about the dire situation with food. 'We tried fishing,' Annie said, 'as we hadn't had any meat for weeks. All we had left were beans and rice.'

Beans and rice. I distinctly recall Annie saying this about their food situation. James also said beans and rice in the letter I received from him in November. Which is why when I look back on everything, I'm inclined to believe this all happened in the autumn of 77. It could simply be that they always had a generous supply of beans and rice. A coincidence perhaps?

'A couple of tenders came out but with barely anything on them,' Ellen went on to say.

I worked out that they must have left the ship immediately after the tender went out with the supplies Oonagh and I had bought while I was in Boulogne.

'A plane flew over one day which dropped a box. We thought it might have been emergency supplies or something, but the only thing in there was a note in telling us to stop broadcasting the numbers or we were fired.'

'What?' I couldn't believe it. Surely it was some kind of joke.

'Who sent the plane?'

They shrugged and mentioned a name but I expressed my doubt, surprise and disbelief. I knew the Dutch regularly sent planes over to drop pre-recorded tapes, but this was something else.

'It's true,' Annie said. 'I'm never going out there again.'

'Me either,' Ellen said.

'Do you have any money for us?' Annie asked.

'No, I wasn't expecting you. I might be able to get you some tomorrow though.'

I invited them to crash out in my living room and did manage to pick up some money for them the following evening after visiting Ronan and explaining the situation.

* * *

Within another day or so of meeting up with Ellen and Annie, everything fell apart in France. Oonagh was arrested and deported. Her French bank accounts were frozen and she couldn't access any of the money there. That meant she lost all her personal funds as well as any Caroline funds. It didn't seem right that she lost her personal income, but I guess the authorities took the view that those earnings had been gained by illegal means.

Attempting to send a tender from France was no longer an option. We had to find an alternative.

Ronan said he would sort out the bulk supply ship but tasked me with finding someone willing to take emergency supplies from England and a changeover of staff. The DJs and crew on board had been out there for months by this time. Way longer than the normal six weeks we planned for (which didn't always go smoothly).

I started at Harwich and worked my way down the coast. Most boat owners I approached shook their heads negatively. I was worried that one of them might report me. Finally, at a small port in Essex, I found someone. His name was Terry – I subsequently learned that it was his father's boat. We were to use them several more times. The boat was a fishing trawler and Terry wanted us to leave port roughly at the time they would if they went fishing.

Between Ronan and I we assembled a take-over crew of several presenters, a cook and an engineer – the famous Peter Chicago. I had never met Peter as he resided in the

Netherlands with Ellen and usually travelled out to the ship on Dutch tenders. At this point he and Ellen had split up. They all turned up at my place ready to leave.

I had done a run to Smithfield meat market to buy bulk supplies of meat, plus bought other food. I couldn't remember how we all travelled to the port with everyone plus the supplies as I still had my little Morris 1000, but Peter Chicago reminded me that he followed me in another car with further bodies and supplies. James was to drive it back to my place once the exchange had been completed. I had two cars at the time – I'd bought a Rover 100 as I'd always wanted one and after realising it was too expensive for me to drive around town (as it guzzled petrol) I later sold it to Peter.

I hung around the port waiting to see if they made it as the weather wasn't looking too good. They had to turn back. We offered some of the fresh meat to Terry and his crew and took the rest back to my place. We set a new date for a further attempt a week later. Most of the presenters lived too far away to return home – they also couldn't afford to travel long distances so I ended up with a load of bodies crashing in my living room.

With so much meat, the cook, Jeff, set about making us some tasty meals before it went off. I didn't have a freezer back then, only a small under-the counter refrigerator with a freezer compartment. Simon thought it was fabulous having so many men around and the novelty of a man cooking for us. I found it very noisy. There was non-stop chatter, something I wasn't used to in my home. I was used to the sound of the radio or music (played fairly loud) as I always had a decent record player but I didn't have a television at the time. They chatted instead.

The following week I had to travel down to Smithfield to buy another large quantity of meat. Any that wouldn't fit into the fridge, was left in the kitchen overnight.

We set out on a Saturday morning and this time I decided to go with them as Simon was spending the day with Brenda and Claudia. I'd never been out to the ship and thought, after working for Radio Caroline for some years, it was about time I made the effort.

The weather forecast wasn't brilliant but Terry set off, optimistic that we could make it. The sea turned rougher as we progressed. I'm not a brilliant sailor at the best of times, but this journey was proving challenging. We hit force gale winds.

Terry announced that we've have to turn back as the sea was too rough. He said we wouldn't be able to unload our cargo or change the crew; it was too dangerous. He told us to stay inside the cabin. I couldn't. It stunk of seafood and oil. I'm allergic to seafood and the smell of it also makes me ill. Despite it being very dangerous to be out on deck, I clung to the railings where every now and then my stomach heaved. Jeff did the same. I warned him not to stand downwind from me. He was too preoccupied to heed my advice and at one unfortunate moment when I released my stomach contents, a gust of wind caught it, slamming it into Jeff's face. Poor man.

Back at port we once again divided the meat between us and Terry's crew. We were unable to set a new date

to try again as the forecast was going to be bad for days
to come.

13

The bodies at my flat thinned out a little after one of them declared he'd had enough following the second aborted attempt. He set off up north for home. The others remained.

Even after passing some onto my friends, we still had an excess of meat hanging around the flat that was starting to smell. It would have been too rank to take back out to the ship so we decided to bury it in my garden. There was a lot of it. After wrapping it in black bin liners a couple of us carried it up to the back of the garden where we dug a hole and buried it. The hole we dug wasn't that deep but we wanted it deep enough so that it wouldn't give off an odour, attract rats, or the wild cats who lived around there.

New meat was purchased for the third trip. I dropped them at the port and returned home. Once again, the second car must have been left there for them.

Shortly after I arrived back from the port, the police knocked on my door.

'We've had a report about you burying something

in your garden,' they said. 'Can we ask you what that was?'

Shit! I was chewing an apple and took my time swallowing a mouthful before answering to give me time to decide what I was going to say.

'It was rotten meat. Mainly beef. I'd planned to have a large barbeque with my friends last weekend but as the weather wasn't good enough, we weren't able to. My friends took some of the meat, but I still had an excessive amount. None of us have freezers, so it went off.'

'Do you mind if we have a look?' they asked.

I did mind but thought it might seem suspicious if I said no.

I led them through the flat and out into the garden, collecting my spade on the way. I expected them (there were two of them in uniforms) to do the digging but they stood waiting for me to do it.

After exposing a section of the bin liners, one of them knelt down and ripped a bit of it open. I could smell the meat from where I stood so it must have been pretty gross for him. He turned and nodded at his companion.

'Beef,' he said. He stood and they thanked me saying they needn't bother me any further.

'Did you think it might be a dead body?' I asked them.

'Something like that was reported to us,' one of them said nodding.

I knew who would have made that report. I saw the police out, looking up at my next-door neighbour's house on the way. The window was in darkness. An elderly woman lived next door on the raised ground floor. She had a clear view of my garden and I'd often noticed her sitting at the window looking out. I used to wave to her but she never waved back. I believe she owned a ginger cat I knew was called Humphrey. I'd seen it on her window ledge and heard her calling him. A couple of years prior, when I had a basset hound called Ben in the flat, Humphrey used to lay on the top of the brick wall that divided my garden and next door's, driving Ben crazy as it was much too high for him to reach. The same neighbour would then lean out of her window shouting at Ben to shut up. It was guaranteed that the minute I let Ben out into the garden, Humphrey would appear and lounge across the top of the fence.

The dog was abandoned with me by my ex-boss (who had taken off to New Zealand) and I spent many months trying to find a home for him as I didn't want another dog. I already had one that had been dumped on me some years prior. Ben had been gone for a good couple of years by the time the police visited me. Humphrey was still about but he didn't lounge on the fence any more – probably due to the wild cats that had installed themselves under my house.

I imagine that at some point someone in the neighbourhood moved away and left a couple of cats behind. The cats bred and the numbers multiplied. They looked very unhealthy, had weeping eyes and wouldn't let anyone near them. I called an animal charity and when they came to collect them my elderly neighbour (Humphrey's owner) and another woman objected to the charity removing them. The charity said that if anyone objected, they couldn't proceed. Apparently, they would have put the cats down as they were so sick. The neighbour knew who they were due to their name being listed on the side of their van. I tried a second charity with the same results. When I finally moved out of the flat the following year, the cats, with ever increasing numbers, were still there.

Late that night James turned up on my doorstep looking filthy dirty. The exchange of staff had been successful. The first thing I made him do was strip off and take a bath.

Bit by bit he revealed how dire things had been. One of the staff became so desperate, he launched the rubber dinghy and rowed off into the sunset. They had to call the lifeguard to rescue him. I don't know if the person in question was arrested.

From this point on regular tenders or crew exchanges with Caroline staff were made from the English coast.

14

The problem with 'cash' and Caroline was that the money was illegal in the UK. If anyone stole 'Caroline' money, no legal proceedings could be launched against them. Ronan wasn't the type to send any heavies after the person in question (even if he knew where to find enforcing thugs). So, from time-to-time money disappeared that had an impact on everyone who was expecting to be paid.

I knew produce intended for the ship was pilfered. I'd heard about someone taking off with the tender money once. But I only know of two occasions when larger sums were stolen. Money similar to amounts I collected from Amsterdam or Lichtenstein. It may have happened on other occasions – Ronan didn't like people knowing about it. I knew about these two instances because he had to tell me due to the surrounding circumstances in which they occurred.

My runs to Amsterdam or Lichtenstein came to an end once I started working for the toiletry bag company after completing my higher education studies. In the first little while I wasn't in a position to travel to Europe with my broken foot. Then I wasn't prepared to take time off.

Whoever did the trips had to be available on a weekday. I seem to remember Ronan telling me the Amsterdam bank option I'd used was no longer available and the money had to be collected by other means. I don't know how he organised it. Perhaps he found another bank.

One day when I went to Ronan's to collect money it became apparent that he'd just had a meeting with Joanna who'd not long left him. I surmised that she'd just returned from a money collecting run.

'What is it with women and fur coats?' he growled.

'I don't know what you're talking about.'

'Joanna,' (again not her real name) he said. 'She's just like Oonagh. She turned up here wearing a fur jacket.'

My immediate thoughts were, *how could Joanna afford a fur jacket?*

Oonagh, on the other hand, had always worn fur coats or jackets since I'd known her. They were an integral part of her wardrobe. Fur wasn't so frowned upon so much in those days. Oonagh didn't own winter clothes. She wore her summer dresses all year round and threw a fur coat over them when she went out in the car. She wasn't one for hiking in the countryside.

Joanna, though, had been a student up until the end of the academic year that calendar year and as far as I knew was still doing a few cleaning jobs as well as odd jobs for Ronan. She also had a car. Either she had rich parents (which may have been the case) or she had acquired some dodgy money. I believe Ronan had already used her for a couple of trips to collect large sums. I would have assumed that he would know exactly how much she was supposed to collect and be aware of whether any of it was missing. He had asked her to pay a number of people though so she could have held onto money.

'You must be paying her a fortune then,' I quipped. I was still being paid my pittance of £10 per week while accumulating money for my house purchase. Supposedly.

He frowned. Joanna wouldn't have been providing free labour for Ronan and I suspect he was paying her a lot more than I was receiving. I know Oonagh was always paid a living wage. She needed to partially support herself on what she earned. She had income from tenants, plus Sonny gave her money. Apart from the sum that was paid into the account in Lichtenstein, I knew exactly what Oonagh earned as she always asked me to negotiate any increases. She and Ronan couldn't discuss the matter together without arguing. It had to come through a third party.

Ronan denied he was paying Joanna so much that she could afford a fur coat.

'She must have rich parents then,' I said.

He sat in silence for a few minutes with a thoughtful look on his face.

We concluded our business and I left.

A month or so later I was at Ronan's flat again to collect

wages.

'Joanna hasn't delivered the money,' he said, looking worried. 'And I don't know how to get hold of her. Do you think something's happened to her?'

My antenna rose a notch. There was something wrong here.

'What time was she supposed to be here?'

'Late last night, but she phoned and said she'd come over today instead as she was so tired.'

'Don't you have her phone number?' I asked him.

He claimed to have lost it and hadn't memorised it. 'Besides, she usually calls me.'

'Okay. What time was she supposed to come today?'

'This morning.'

It was evening by this time. I realised I knew her number. I'd only called her a couple of times but numbers stuck in my head. I used to be very good with anything that involved numbers: timetables for buses and trains, bus numbers and their routes, dates, sums of money, car registration plates or phone numbers.

'I think I know her number,' I said. I reached for his phone and dialled. Joanna answered. Her voice sounded hesitant.

'Joanna. It's Lyn here,' I said. 'Ronan was expecting you to be at his place this morning.'

'*What? I don't know what you're talking about,*' she said. Her tone was defensive and hostile.

'You did a collection for him yesterday.' I was being cautious about what I said over the phone in case people were listening.

'*No, I didn't.*'

'Joanna, stop it. We're talking about peoples' lives here.'

'*I've got to go now,*' she said and hung up. I tried calling back, but she didn't pick up.

I relayed what Joanna had said to Ronan.

'She definitely collected the money yesterday,' he said.

'I'm going over to her place,' I told Ronan.

'You know where she lives then? Because I don't.'

'Yes, I've been there once. I'm sure I can find it. How much were you expecting her to deliver to you?'

'Ten thousand.'

I remember thinking then that it was a good thing that she hadn't done a larger run as I suspected we might have trouble getting the money off her. I was going to do my best to ensure we did though.

Ronan looked nervous and worried.

'You're sure about this? That it was Joanna you sent?'

'*Of course* I'm sure.'

He appeared to be telling the truth and I was inclined to believe him. I'd always mistrusted Joanna. I'm not sure why.

I jumped into my car and drove over to her flat. There was no answer even though I left my thumb pressing the bell continuously. I managed to get in through the front door after someone exited the property and reached her flat door. No one answered to my knock. I peered underneath the gap at the bottom of the door and the place seemed to be in darkness. She was either sitting in there in the dark pretending she wasn't home, or she had actually taken off.

It turned out to be the latter. Joanna disappeared from her flat. I made another few attempts to find her at home without success. We never saw her again and, as far as I know, she made no further contact with anyone who worked on Caroline.

Needless to say, staff weren't paid what they were owed. I returned to Ronan's that night to tell him she wasn't answering. He asked me not to tell anyone what had happened with Joanna. When I asked him why, he said he didn't want it to be commonly known that one of the staff had stolen money. He believed it might put similar ideas into other people's heads. I did refrain from telling most of the staff but I believe I informed Oonagh and James. Oonagh because I guess I was angry that she had hired someone who would do that. I can't recall the outcome of that conversation.

I thought Joanna's theft was bad but the next one, some months later, sent me into a rage. Once again, I called over to Ronan's to collect the wages and discovered that this time the person had taken a huge sum. £50,000.

After Ronan broke the news, I burst into tears of rage. 'How could someone do that!' I screeched. 'Who was it?' I shouted at him. 'Who?'

He mentioned a name. It was someone I had never met, as Ronan always dealt with him in person but he had worked out on the ship for quite some time.

'Where is he? Has he made any contact with you?'

He had apparently. And told Ronan he wasn't returning with the money.

'Has he done this because you owe him a load of money?' I asked Ronan. I knew there were a lot more people besides me who worked for Ronan who were either underpaid or owed money.

He shrugged.

'How could you be so stupid?' I shouted at him. 'To let someone you owe money to collect such a large sum?'

'I didn't have anyone else available to ask. You're not doing it anymore.'

'I can't. So don't even go there,' I shouted at him.

'What do I tell people? Dick and Tim? (David was no longer working on the film at this point). The DJ's? I've got a couple coming around over the weekend.' I *hated* telling DJs that I had no money for them. I hated it so much that a few times I'd paid them part of their money out of my own pocket – although I never told Ronan that – in case he wouldn't reimburse me. I always told him the guys were owed their full amount.

'You can't tell them about this,' he stressed.

Once again, he wanted to keep it quiet. He wouldn't let me leave until I promised to say nothing. I kept my promise while I worked for him, but did talk about it in subsequent years to friends who had nothing to do with Caroline.

With Ronan's death however, I broke my silence on the subject in Caroline circles. People I have told, such as Peter Chicago, found it very difficult to believe that one of his colleagues could have stolen such a large sum. He thought it must have been someone else who had a reputation and track record of stealing. I pointed out that the one we all knew about only amounted to a couple of thousand; money that was intended to cover the cost of a tender.

Peter did admit though, that the person I'd mentioned was driving a new flashy car around the time in question and started a business, so it could have been true. He equally thought that perhaps Ronan had lied to me about the money, because some years later when Peter was living on the Ross Revenge in Spain, waiting for money to come through for repairs, Ronan told a number of people that it was Peter's fault that the ship wasn't ready to launch again, rather than admit he hadn't been able to raise the money to cover the costs. Ronan didn't hesitate to use scapegoats to cover his tracks at times. He did it to me with George Harrison.

Ronan *could* have lied to me. If so, he was a brilliant actor. He seemed very distressed about the whole incident. There's no evidence to prove what Ronan told me. I only know we had no money in the coffers for quite a while.

The thing I found astounding out of the whole episode was that Ronan hired the man in question to go back onto the ship some months later. When I heard he was back out there, I asked Ronan what on earth he thought he was doing, hiring this man again.

'There's method in my madness,' he said. He told me he needed this man's skills and had no one else available.

Ronan had *persuaded* the man to go back out. But he had
no intention of paying him ever again he told me.

15

The theft of large sums of money from the Caroline coffers caused Ronan some distress, anxiety, anger and frustration. It didn't cause him to cry. I knew of only one incident that led to him shedding tears.

With no children of his own (that he was aware of, he once clarified), Ronan took the children of some of his friends to heart. He did it with my son Simon for a time. Every time I saw him, he'd ask about Simon if he hadn't seen him for a while.

One of Ronan's good friends had a daughter called Tracey, who often accompanied her father when they met up. Ronan acted as though he was a proud father when she developed into a beautiful young girl. He mentioned her often when I met with him. Always in a paternal manner.

I met Tracey only the once at Ronan's flat, shortly before her eighteenth birthday. She was beautiful and not just in appearances. Although by the time she turned eighteen she was a stunner, she also radiated beauty with her personality.

One day when I turned up to Ronan's he blurted out, 'Tracey's dead,' And promptly burst into tears. I too, started crying.

'How?' I asked him.

'A heroin overdose,' he told me through his choking tears. This shocked me as Tracey was the last person I would have expected to indulge in heroin. Apparently, it was the one and only time she had ever taken it. As a novice, she had no idea of its potency and had injected too much.

Ronan wasn't the type of person who I would hug on greeting and parting. We had established a friendly distance in our working relationship. That day though I intuitively wanted to rush over and comfort him. Before I had the chance to do so he exploded with anger.

Although he didn't partake in any type of drug (including alcohol), Ronan didn't seem to have any issues with those who did. I was a smoker and occasionally he'd say, 'those cigarettes will kill you.' But he never veered into lengthy lectures about the evils of a given drug.

That day he went into a raging fury directed at Tracey's father, whom he knew took drugs. Tracey had been exposed to them at parties throughout her short life Ronan claimed. He blamed his friend. I sat listening to him in silence, letting him vent his anger.

Needless to say, there was little work done that day. Whatever I had gone over there to discuss with him was shelved.

As the weeks and months passed, Ronan's hostility

towards Tracey's father deepened and their friendship came to an end.

There were murmurings in Caroline circles that Ronan might have had his eye on Tracey as a potential lover. I don't think for a moment that was the case. Whilst Ronan's eye wandered when he spotted an attractive woman and he would use a range of strategies to approach and woo them for his own needs, Tracey didn't fit into that category. He considered her a child still when she died and was heartbroken at the tragic and needless loss of her life.

16

After all the upheavals in the autumn of 1977, James was back on the ship in February 1978. We were still seeing each other.

In his letter dated February 78 it appears that a reporter from the Evening News had been out to the ship and interviewed him.

It seems that all went well on that trip. Some of his comments included:

'On Sunday 12th February we (James and Mark Lawrence) stayed up all night working on the extension to the Library.' (record library)

Apparently, I'd written a letter to staff and crew which was read out. I don't remember doing so and there is little reference to its contents. He says:

'Everyone realised you were acting as a messenger.' (?? Sounds ominous)

On Sunday 19th February they had to ring the coastguard to tell them all was well.

'The sea had been really rough and the ship was bouncing all over the place.'

In a later letter dated March '78 James says:

'The foreign organisers came on the other day saying all we play is science fiction and drug orientated music.'

Really? What would they have preferred? Records from the pop charts of the day? By then Caroline was playing album tracks. Not songs from the pop charts. Other radio stations were doing that. 'Science fiction and drug orientated music' was clearly the 'foreign organisers' reaction to rock music that was being played along with a wide range of other music – including the Beatles.

James mentions that new lino had been laid on the floor in the mess room. A cupboard was built and the mess painted, plus curtains erected.

Sounds like they were making it more homely.

He says: 'the food on board has improved with a different cook.'

The weather was very good.

James helped to install a new electric oven/cooker.

'We accidentally plugged it into the 400-volt supply and fused everything.'

Once it was sorted, he says: 'Everything cooks very fast now.'

A small tender came from the English side but there were no goodies (treats) much to everyone's disappointment.

I sent another letter out to the ship saying RE was coming out to sort things out (whatever that meant). Apparently, the news disturbed everyone.

That was the final trip that James made to the ship. He decided he wanted to go for a land-based job. He was offered temporary work at Swansea Sound radio. Simon and I joined him down there briefly and considered what we might do if he was offered a permanent position. Sadly, the job didn't work out.

I no longer made personal visits to tender owners. Terry, who had I'd set up to do runs from Essex did several more for us. I'd phone him to organise dates, arrange change-over staff, then give a trusted staff member the money to pay him. I don't remember when or why he ceased doing them.

I never had anything to do with the Caroline Road Shows but Ronan spoke to me of them when they were held. I gained the impression he acquired small sums of money from some of these events. One day when I visited him to collect wages, he handed me a Caroline Road Show sweatshirt which he said he'd requested as a present for Simon. It was miles too big for him at the time but he hung onto it and wore it over the years.

I told Ronan I didn't have the time to do both the Caroline work *and* the film work. I was working during the day and many evenings were taken up with work for Ronan. Oonagh also called me most nights and we had extended calls. She was no longer working for Ronan.

Ronan had no one else to do the film work, whereas he could always find someone to pull in for Caroline. It was with much regret that I had to let Caroline go – at that point at least.

17

In the spring of 1978 Ronan called me to a meeting about the film.

'I want you to set up a screening at our usual place so show potential investors part one of the film,' he said. Our usual screening theatre was in Wardour Street in the West End.

'Sure, I can organise it, but I won't necessarily be able to attend. You'll have to have Dick or Tim turn up with the film.'

The screening went ahead one afternoon. I tried to organise it for 4pm but Ronan wanted it shown early in the afternoon. It may have been on this screening that James operated the sound on the film for Ronan. He did it a few times – but never when I was there. He recently recalled the enjoyment of whacking the volume to the max when rockets were launched in the opening scenes.

I didn't know who Ronan had invited to the screening, but I was soon to find out when he called me over for a further meeting.

'George is finally interested in investing in the film,'

he told me. 'I've been trying to persuade him for some time.'

I knew this time around he was talking about George Harrison. It was then I realised what Ronan's agenda had been the year before. He'd wanted me to get to know George and talk to him about the film; another angle of pressure. When I challenged him about this, he admitted it would have been useful for me to talk to George while staying at his place.

'And I have Tony Summers willing to interview our witnesses in America,' Ronan went on to say.

Tony, was better known as Anthony Summers. He'd worked for some years on Panorama, a news/documentary show screened on the BBC. He'd jointly written a book with Tom Mangold – his co-presenter on Panorama called, *The File on the Tsar* (which being interested in history, I'd read). It was well written. Ronan and I had discussed the book so he knew I'd know who he was talking about.

'Tony wants to write a book about JFK and I've persuaded him to do our interviews on the understanding he can use some of what the witnesses say and other parts of our research in his book.'

It all sounded very promising. We'd reached a point with the film where we couldn't progress any further without carrying out interviews of witnesses we'd tracked down. Money was also in short supply. We'd raised some money by sub-licencing some of our footage to ITV for a documentary they were making about JFK to be released later that year (on the 25th anniversary of his death). It had taken some weeks to sort out and necessitated me attending various meetings at their studios of a late afternoon (I refused to go during my working day which was still 9.30 to 3.00pm) before the deal was struck. I recently found a bank paying-in book for REF that showed a payment of £500 from Thames TV. Whether this was a deposit or the total sum of what they paid us I can't recall. I do know the money we made was quickly absorbed and we didn't have the money to complete the film. To cut costs Ronan had asked me to let David go. There was only Dick, Tim and I left. And Tim was having to take on other work as we couldn't afford to pay him every week.

'I'd like you to draw up a budget to complete the film and then you can set up a meeting with George and Dennis.'

'Dennis?' I queried. Was Dennis George's solicitor I wondered.

'Dennis O'Brien, he's George's manager. They're investing together. How soon could you do it?' he asked me. Ronan always wanted everything done yesterday. He forgot that some people had other commitments such as a job and a family.

'That depends on other information I'll require. Are we hiring a crew from the UK to fly out with this Tony? Or are we hiring them in the US? What about Dick? Will he be going? Presumably you will be paying Tony for his services. What sum of money have you agreed on? How long do you think they'll need to be there? Is he willing to fly economy? I'd have to cost in all those factors.'

'Tony wants to take a film crew from here. Dick will be going – to direct everything. Don't worry about all those costs. Just make it all up to look impressive.'

It was typical of Ronan to want to skate over the details.

'I'll do it within the next few days,' I told him. I knew I would be working on it at home after my day job – once Simon was in bed.

'Can't you do it any faster?'

'No. Not if it's to be done properly. We're only talking about a budget to complete part two to a rough cut, aren't we?'

'Yes, yes, but we don't need to tell George that.'

Ronan might not tell George but I would.

I had a friend in the business so obtained costings for a cameraman and sound engineer. After talking to Dick and learning that the witnesses were in various locations around America, I had to include travel within the US and accommodation for approximately six weeks. Then there was the cost of putting it all together back in the UK and completing part two – which Dick and Tim had started.

I finished the budget, rounding it up to about £150,000. When I turned up at Ronan's with it, he almost had a breakdown.

'No, no. You can't give that to George. He won't put the money in if you do. Go back and cut it down to fifty thousand.'

'Fifty thousand is totally unrealistic Ronan. Have you been lying to George telling him it would only cost around that much?'

He wouldn't say, but I could tell that was exactly what he'd done.

'The way these things work is that you hook them in with a much lower amount than what it will really be. Once they've invested their money they will want to put more in, otherwise they stand to lose their investment. We can go back to him for more money when our fifty-thousand runs out.'

I didn't think this was a good way to conduct business and told him so. We argued about it until he said, 'It works. I should know. I've been doing business this way for years.'

And ducking and diving endless investors in his projects, I didn't add. How was that successful?

Ronan truly believed this film was going to be a huge box office success. That millions of people around the world would want to see it (and he would make loads of money). I believed it could have moderate box office success.

'I'm not prepared to sit in a meeting with George and Dennis and lie,' I told him.

'It's the only way,' he said. 'Re-do it as I've asked.'

I was sceptical about his strategy but I did re-do it, rounding it down to £50,000. I then had my first meeting with George and Dennis.

'Are you sure that this is all it's going to cost?' George asked me.

'It will get us through to the next stage,' I said. I was very careful with the language I used, hoping they would read between the lines.

'But you will be able to finish the film, as Ronan claims after doing these interviews?'

'We'll have all the footage we'll need for the film, yes,' I said. That was technically correct. With the US interviews we would have all the footage we needed. It then had to be sifted through and the best bits chosen for inclusion in part two. Part two centred largely around the investigation into JFK's assassination.

George and Dennis seemed pleased. I don't think they listened carefully enough to what I was saying. They agreed we'd meet again to sign documents. They asked me to draw up contracts stating what percentage of profits they'd receive. Dennis told me they were forming a film company to invest in this project. It was to be called 'Hand Made Films.'

On the odd occasion I mentioned my connection to the film and George Harrison, friends often asked if I wasn't 'starstruck' or in awe of him. The answer is 'No.' I held a high regard for him and loved the Beatles music (plus much of their later individual music). In the second half of 60s as a teenager I worked part-time for one of Sydney's top entertainer promoters. At the office or in one of my bosses' nightclubs, meeting and socialising with 'stars' became an everyday occurrence for me. My day job (which my father bullied me into doing after plans to attend art college collapsed) was training in accounts so the entertainment world I encountered of an evening and at weekends made life more interesting.

At my next meeting with George and Dennis, all documentation was signed. Before they signed on the dotted line I said, 'you do know that this will only enable us to work towards a rough-cut finish of part two, don't you?'

'Yes,' Dennis said. 'But it will be finished then?'

Did they not understand what a rough-cut meant?

'To a rough cut, yes.' Fingers crossed that we could get that far.

As it turned out there was no way we were going to make it to a rough cut. Tony Summers decided he wanted a renowned French film crew to travel with him. They cost twice as much as the crew I budgeted for. He'd failed to mentioned this little fact to Ronan at the outset of negotiations. When Tony had told him he was taking a local crew, Ronan assumed he meant a British one. I would have thought the same. But I think Tony meant a French crew who *worked* in England. Even though I picked up a deal on flights, they also cost more than I'd estimated. They wanted to fly with Pan Am. I'd set prices with a different company. Already costs were creeping up.

George and Dennis sent the first instalment of money

to the Film company's (REF) bank account. I paid for everything and the crew set off for the US. On one-way tickets. They weren't sure how long it was going to take so return flights would be booked as the finishing line approached. The money quickly ran out and I asked for more. Another advance came in using up nearly all the money George and Dennis were due to invest. I'd told Ronan the money was nearly gone – reminding him that the crew Tony had wanted was costlier. Ronan had agreed to Tony's costlier team, otherwise he claimed Tony would have pulled out. I warned Ronan that he needed to approach George pretty soon, and persuade them to part with more money or we'd be in trouble. He said he would.

While our Director, Dick, was away filming in America, he had asked Ronan and me to keep an eye on his wife and son who he'd left behind at Elvaston Place. Dick's wife, Pat, was not a well woman. His son Smokey was only about 6 years old, a year younger than my son Simon. Simon and Smokey had met several times as Simon accompanied me to Elvaston some weeks. At one point, Smokey contracted mumps and so I took Simon over to expose him to it. I wanted him to catch mumps while he was young. Although Simon played with Smokey all day, he didn't catch the mumps. Neither I, nor my brother had mumps as children, so perhaps we had some natural immunity to it.

I'd been calling into Elvaston once a week to check all was well and I'd often take food. Sometimes Simon would accompany me so Smokey had someone to play with. If Pat was in bed, I'd cook us all a meal. I knew Dick had other friends also checking on them. Smokey seemed okay so I had to assume everything was fine.

I received a call from Ronan one day to say the electricity was due to be cut off at Elvaston and a bill needed paying. It amounted to almost £250. That was *a lot* of money in those days. After collecting the bill, I called into an LEB (London Electricity Board) office to find out why a bill this high had been sent.

It transpired that the electricity at Elvaston should have been disconnected some years prior. The termination notice, along with those of several other households had been placed in a desk drawer to be dealt with. The person who was dealing with them for some reason never returned to work at LEB. Whether the person responsible had died suddenly wasn't clear. The desk was moved to a store room without anyone searching its contents. When the storeroom was being cleared out someone did check the drawers and discovered the termination notices. Upon investigation it was discovered that no further bills had been issued to 16 Elvaston. Someone was sent out to read the meter and they realised that a further considerable debt had accumulated. The bill had to be paid or the electricity would definitely be cut off this time. I argued that it was unreasonable to expect a customer to pay such a high bill in one go and attempted to negotiate monthly instalments. They wouldn't agree to this so I paid the bill – out of the film account as it was our base for the film – using virtually the last of the money George and

Dennis had so far invested.

I had a key for going in and out of Elvaston that Dick had given me. When I returned to Elvaston to let them know the electricity bill had been paid Pat was in bed. Smokey was playing in his bedroom. I decided to check how the gas was dealt with. I asked Smokey, not sure if he'd be able to tell me anything but he was a very smart, bright little boy. He led me upstairs and showed me the meter. It was a pay meter which ten pence coins had to be inserted into. The coin box was not sealed and there was a solitary ten pence piece in there. Smokey picked it up and put it through the pay slot. After it dropped down, he picked it up and ran it through again. He did this several times before turning to me and smiling.

'This is how we pay for the gas,' he said. I wondered if he realised that they were receiving free gas and what the story was as to how this had come about.

I cooked Smokey (and Pat) some food that day before I left.

Today, Smokey is a successful writer, producer and Digital Entrepreneur in the States. I believe Dick took the family to America shortly after the filming there. His wife Pat, was American and came from New York. I know Dick wasn't around a couple of years later. How long he remained there I don't know as he no longer had anything to do with our film. Dick had had a successful career prior to working with Ronan and he subsequently went on to have further successes in both the US and the UK.

The film crew in America were many weeks into the

schedule when Ronan called me over for a meeting and dropped a bombshell.

18

The bombshell was that George and Dennis would not be putting any more money into the film. Not for the time being at least.

I had to put a hand over my mouth, close my lips tightly and look away to avoid exploding with anger. Not against George or Dennis but with Ronan. I guess he picked up on this. He knew how much I was against presenting an unrealistic budget. After a while he said it wasn't his strategy that was at fault (he would say that of course) – it was because George had committed himself heavily elsewhere.

The story Ronan told me – which George supposedly explained to him, was that George had bumped into Terry Gillam (of the Monty Python group) in Los Angles. Terry had casually asked George what he was up to these days. George told him about the creation of Hand Made Films and the film he'd invested in. At that time the Monty Python group had started on the *Life of Brian*. They were unable to finish it because they'd run out of money. Terry asked George if he'd be willing to invest in their film and he readily agreed. The kind of money required exceeded ready cash that George had available. So, he apparently borrowed against his home to raise the necessary funds. George didn't have a dime to spare for our film.

'George wasn't happy to hear that we'd run out of money before the crew had even returned from America,' Ronan added.

'And I suppose you told him that I had grossly underestimated all the costs,' I said.

Ronan didn't reply but had that sheepish look on his face I'd seen many times before. I knew that was *exactly* what he would have told George. Passing the buck. Blaming someone else.

'How are we going to get the film crew back then?' I asked. 'Can you raise the money elsewhere?' I meant from a loan from one of his wealthy business friends. He thought I meant from Radio Caroline income.

'We're barely covering our costs as it is on Caroline. I can't use any of that income.'

I didn't think costs *were* being covered on Caroline at that particular juncture. The DJs were owed considerable sums, not to mention supplies that were needed for the ship. Although I agreed that he shouldn't take any money from the Caroline pot, it was almost laughable that Ronan should say this. Radio Caroline revenue had been supporting the film for *years*.

'I didn't mean that. What about your business friends?'

He shook his head. In other words: 'No'.

In the days that followed I made a stab at approaching some of his business acquaintances myself over at the Casserole Restaurant. None were interested. In desperation I raised the subject with Ronan again. 'Don't you know *anyone* who might be able to help?' I asked. 'We have a film crew over in America who we need to fly back,' I reminded him.

'I know, I know.'

He sat in thoughtful silence for a few minutes before saying, 'There might be someone.'

The *someone* did turn out to be one his business acquaintances; one I'd not met before. Ronan asked me to draw up yet another budget claiming we could complete the film for £20,000 and a contract giving this man a small percentage of profits from the UK sales – i.e. almost the same as Hand Made Films. I was not happy about this and Ronan and I argued yet again. This man was only putting in £20,000!

'He's our only hope of getting the film crew back and processing all the footage,' he reminded me.

'You could have asked for more so that we could finish the film properly,' I said.

'That's all he could do.'

I wondered if this was true or whether Ronan had used his usual approach and claimed £20,000 was all that we needed to finish the film.

When I asked Ronan where I was to meet this guy with the contract he said, 'I've told him that you will meet up with him for dinner – at his expense of course. So, dress up, be nice to him and make sure he signs the contract.'

'What do you mean by "be nice" to him?' I asked. Warning bells were ringing in my ears.

'Just be *nice* to him. And reassure him that we can finish the film with his money.'

We met in an expensive swanky restaurant. I imagined that 'call girls' felt much as I did that night as I introduced myself and we were shown to a table. The man wasn't one of Ronan's business mates I'd seen at the Casserole restaurant. He was of a similar ilk though. Middle-aged, overweight with hair receding.

As the meal progressed, I came to the conclusion that he was a very nice man. He made no improper suggestions towards me – unlike some of the Casserole crowd. He seemed very enthusiastic about the film and we spent most of the evening talking about it. I can't recall whether he had been to a screening and seen part one. The big question was would he sign the documents? That proved to be no problem and I felt sorry for him as he committed his signature to paper, wondering if he'd ever get his money back.

I asked him whether he was going to organise a bank transfer into the film's account. He mentioned that Ronan had suggested he pay part cash, part cheque.

Ronan would, thinking he could keep hold of the cash.

'Definitely no cash,' I said. 'I'd rather a cheque for the full amount that I can pay into the bank.'

He seemed happy with this and wrote me a cheque there and then for £20,000. I felt like a fraudster as we parted company. At least with the money going into the bank, it would be used for it intended purpose.

I deposited the cheque the next day and informed Ronan that I'd been paid the full amount.

'It's all gone into the bank?' he asked, sounding disappointed.

'Of course. And it's only going to be used for the film Ronan,' I stressed. He didn't say anything.

I was able to fly the crew back, pay them off and have the hours of footage shot processed. I catalogued the details. I also had the sound track transferred to tapes so that transcripts could be typed up for all the interviews. I have a vague recollection of Oonagh helping me with this mammoth task. There were 396 takes (I still have the slate shoot list) – most with considerable dialogue. Oonagh was no longer on the payroll by then, but we were paid properly for our labours (for once). I spent many weeks working at night on this task.

That's as far as it went then. No further progress was made on part two.

I know Ronan and Dick spoke a few times. Ronan didn't enlighten me on the conversations that took place. I only know neither Dick, nor Tim would be doing any further work on the film. Unless we had a further cash injection, it seemed unlikely that the film would be completed.

19

Having control of the bank account for the film company, I thought I was safe from any of Ronan's shenanigans. How wrong I was.

Unbeknown to me, he ran up a £5000 debt in the film company's name connected to his Caroline Homes project. Working with Sonny (Oonagh's husband), Ronan had designed a modular house which he believed would help to solve the housing crisis. Hackney council was interested in placing an order for a substantial number of them and had installed one in the borough for people to view.

Ronan had attempted to drag me into his Caroline Homes project. I found it interesting – anything to do with houses interests me but I simply didn't have the time.

I'd wanted to be an architect when I was still at school but the careers advisor politely informed me that it wasn't a career for women – only men. I wasn't allowed to do technical drawing at school – only the boys could – although I managed to escape Religious Studies (RS) classes by forging a note from my father saying we were atheists so I could attend the technical drawing classes that ran during the weekly RS sessions.

I also knew Ronan would expect me to put in additional, and no doubt, unpaid hours for Caroline Homes which I wasn't prepared to do.

The Caroline Home structure was made of a specific type of concrete mix and, according to Ronan, the debt he ran up was for the purchase of materials to make further sample modules. He claimed the materials they supplied were faulty, they'd not been able to use them and so he wasn't prepared to pay for it. Rather than dealing with the issue through legal means, he simply ignored it – until a court order appeared. If he didn't appeal it by a certain date, a judgement would be passed and the £5000 would have to be paid.

I had no knowledge of this company's invoice as Ronan used a different address for it. It still beggar's belief that he was able to charge the concrete mix order to the film company. Surely the supplier must have thought it strange and either should have queried it or requested the order in writing with official letterheading. I had always used letters when placing orders on the film. But as per usual, Ronan did all his blagging in person or over the phone.

The first I knew of it was when he phoned me early in the morning to say he had court papers which had to be lodged that day by 5pm at the Royal Courts of Justice in Fleet Street. I knew the courts as they weren't far from where my office had been located when working for IPC

Magazines.

Ronan asked me to fill the papers in and lodge them at the court. I was getting ready to drop Simon at school and head off to work. I couldn't take a day off at such short notice. I told him to find someone else to do it. Until that moment I thought the debt was in the name of Caroline Homes. It was then he dropped the bombshell that it was in the name of the film company. I almost screamed at him. I agreed to take half a day off and head over to his place with my portable typewriter (to type up the defence on the form). He promised to give me his full attention while we completed the forms. He didn't. The phone kept going and he continued to answer it until I shouted at him. I had to collect Simon from school before I went to the courts. No one else was able to collect him for me that particular day.

I made a mad dash into town, parked the car and raced into the court building. It's a massive building full of workers in hundreds of offices. Minutes were wasted until I was directed to the right room. There was a small foyer with a large counter closed off by sliding frosted glass. A bell sat on the counter to ring. It was 4.50 pm on a Friday afternoon when I rang that bell. I could see the outline shadow of workers behind the glass. I could also hear them. They were laughing and chatting about their plans for the weekend. They ignored the bell. I rang it again, tapped on the glass and called out 'hello?' They continued to ignore me.

At 5pm a loud ringing sounded through the building, signalling it was time to go home. One of the workers opened the sliding glass partition and said, 'sorry, we're closed now.'

Keeping my anger under check, I reminded her that I had been waiting ten minutes for them to answer me and patiently explained that I had a defence to lodge on a deadline that day.

'Sorry, we're finished for the day. I can't help you,' she said and closed the partition. Another man appeared from behind me and asked me to leave. He wanted to lock the entrance doors to the office.

Simon and I walked out into the very long hallway and I sank to the floor in tears of frustration and rage. Something inside me exploded and I screamed my lungs out while *hundreds* of workers ignored me and rushed past on their way out of the building. Poor old Simon tucked his head down – clearly embarrassed by my behaviour. Within minutes the hallway was empty; the building silent. I had never seen anything like it. I then burst into fits of laughter and couldn't stop. It was all so surreal.

I returned with the papers on the Monday straight after work – this time without Simon. I'd made additions to the defence – stating I had attended on the Friday before the deadline but staff had refused to accept the forms. I later wondered if they'd be reading what I'd written and then maybe they'd bin it. It seems not. The appeal went in our favour but I can't recall the final outcome. I know Ronan never paid anything on it.

145

20

In the late summer of 1978, I left the toiletry bag company and registered with Inner London Education Authority (ILEA) for supply teaching work in division two – which covered Camden and Westminster districts. I'd kept my promise to my boss and remained with him for a year. I was sad to leave the job as it was a great company to work for and my salary excellent. Supply teaching was insecure and not as well paid. If I was unable to work for any reason, I'd have no income. Only the £10 a week I was still being paid by Ronan – most weeks. He didn't always have the cash available for me.

Camden Council also re-housed me into a proper two-bedroom garden flat in West Hampstead around the same time. Although they'd decorated parts of it, there was still much to do there and I spent many weeks undertaking decorating, sanding and varnishing floors and building work (I built a brick fireplace in the living room with a wooden mantle). The only heating was a gas fire in the kitchen/diner. There was an open fireplace space in the living room. I paid a deposit on a lovely Victorian inset and mantle from a salvaging unit in West London but when I went to pay the balance and collect it, they'd shut up shop and disappeared. I didn't have enough money to find another one so I built the brick one.

The first school ILEA allocated me to was a five-minute drive from my flat. During my lunch break I would rush home and put another coat of polyurethane varnish on either the kitchen or living room floors. I would coat three boards, then leave three boards to walk on. Doing it this way was long-winded but it meant that we could still function in the flat. Polyurethane took sixteen plus hours to dry.

Simon's bedroom had to have the usual navy-blue ceiling with stars on it. I loved the flat, but it was cavernous and very cold. I was able to have an open fire in the living-room after building the fireplace, but the rest of the rooms had to be heated with an electric heater which made little impact. We froze as autumn progressed and then winter hit. The winter of 78/79 was the worst the country had experienced for many years.

For some time, I had been considering a house purchase and testing Ronan on the agreement he'd made years before to contribute towards it with my so-called deferred 'savings'. It was soon to be put to the test. At first, I looked at buying a house in East London. My upstairs neighbour Vivien, from the short life property I'd lived in asked me to look at a house she was interested in buying. The house didn't have a functioning kitchen or bathroom so building societies wouldn't lend her the money. I made an appointment with the manager of the branch where I held the REF (film) bank account and accompanied Vivien pointing out to the manager positive aspects of investing in this property. Vivien assured him she would be installing a kitchen and bathroom immediately if she was to buy the property. She was a beautiful 'English Rose' and I think the manager was seduced by her feminine charm. He advanced her the money on condition she completed the promised works as soon as possible. When the house next door became available in similar circumstances some weeks later, I attempted to buy it and approached the same manager. He wouldn't lend me the money saying it was okay to have one house in such a poor condition, but he wasn't prepared to have two. It appeared that helping out Vivien did me a disservice. I didn't have her beauty or coquettish charm either.

London was becoming too pricey for me unless I bought a dilapidated house in the East. I had already started looking at other areas during the summer of '78. I loved Bath, a city I had visited many times when travelling down there at weekends or during school holidays to help my cousin out in his business. Bath was also a little pricey. I considered Bristol but didn't know it so well. One place I had visited often with Simon while in that part of the world, was Frome and we both loved the quaintness of the town. I started looking there and found a house I fell in love with, priced at £7500. I approached Ronan about it. Without a decent fixed income, I would not have been able to raise a mortgage and I didn't know how much Ronan would put towards the purchase.

Ronan was unhappy at the thought of me moving out of London, but when I assured him I'd need to work on the house (in Frome) over time and that I wouldn't move until I had obtained a teaching job down there, he seemed appeased. I also promised him that I could still do work on the film (if we had the money) or Caroline for him. He agreed to arrange documentation saying I had a fixed income through the film company and promised to give me £1500 towards the purchase price and to pay my solicitor's fees. That meant I only had to raise a mortgage of £6000 which I was able to do with his phoney paperwork. I argued that £1500 was insufficient, considering all the work I'd put in for him over the years. He reminded me that REF would make loads of money when the film was completed and launched. I could take what I was owed then. I almost laughed at his ludicrous suggestion as I couldn't see that day ever coming. I was sure that, despite the contract I held with the parent company in Lichtenstein, Ronan would find some way to avoid paying REF any money. I wanted this house purchase though and he claimed he couldn't give me any more at that time. It would be a start.

All seemed to be going smoothly on the purchase when the mother of the woman whom I was buying from in Frome rang me. Her daughter had had a breakdown and was in hospital. Did I want to push the sale through or would I mind waiting? It didn't seem right to force her daughter into signing all the documentation while she was in hospital so I agreed to wait.

On 1st January 1979, Simon, Brenda, Claudia and I battled our way down to my cousin's house outside Bath through snow blizzards and hair-raising driving conditions. I was due in Frome the next day to sign the contract. My cousin was on holiday in the Canary Islands and suggested I could go down and warm the house up for his return in a few days. All the pipes were frozen solid and we were unable to light the boiler. There were several open fireplaces in the house but no wood or coal in stock. Outside in a shed were many large lengths of dry timber but no axe to be found anywhere. So, using a double ended saw that was to hand, Brenda and I spent hours slicing through the timber to make firewood. We also, with the children, scooped up loads of snow to warm in pots on the electric cooker and throw over the external pipes. We didn't even have a fresh water supply to the house with these pipes being frozen. We lit several open fires with the timber we'd cut. Eventually the house and frozen pipes thawed and we were able to light the boiler for the central heating.

The next morning, we made our way to Frome. Although the weather had improved a little, the journey was slow.

Ronan was supposed to be wiring the £1500 deposit that day. When I arrived at the solicitor's office in Frome, he told me my house owner had refused to exchange contracts. He didn't know why and suggested I went around to see her. The money from Ronan hadn't come through. The solicitor was due to phone him when he was ready for the exchange – which of course he hadn't done as yet.

When I arrived at the house, the woman's boyfriend wouldn't allow me to see or talk to her. He was an unpleasant large bully who said I couldn't buy the house unless I paid double the price. £15,000. He told me that the house next door was up for sale for £15,000 and that prices were going up all over the town. When I pointed out that the house next door had been completely refurbished and had central heating, he dismissed this as a reason why I shouldn't pay double. I was unable to pay double (and wouldn't have done so on principle) so the sale collapsed.

I know Ronan was overjoyed when the Frome sale fell through – although he pretended to be disappointed on my behalf when we next met. When I asked him to give me the £1500 so I could put it into my savings account he said, 'Wait until you find somewhere else you want to buy. Then I'll give it to you.'

My heart sank. I suspected the money would never be forthcoming. It would be put to the test again later that year.

In May 1979 a Conservative Government was elected with Margaret Thatcher as its leader. She introduced the 'Right to Buy' scheme for council tenants.

I felt quite conflicted about this issue. On the one hand I thought it was great that Council tenants could buy their homes at a reduced rate. Instead of pouring their hard- earned money into rent over decades, they could now acquire an asset that would give them greater social mobility. Hitherto when a council tenant wanted to move to another part of the country, they had to participate in a council house swap scheme, if they wanted to retain the housing security they enjoyed. It wasn't always successful. If they owned their own homes, it meant they could sell it and buy somewhere else – if their means permitted.

However, the Conservatives had no intention of replacing the depleted public housing stock. I knew this would lead to a housing shortage which was already clearly in evidence. Housing Associations were starting to spring up around the country providing a service which councils had traditionally filled. With the decimation of public housing, families who couldn't afford to buy would become more reliant on private landlords – who charged much higher rents. I suspected this was what the Tories were aiming for in the long term.

I made tentative enquiries about the situation if I bought my West Hampstead council flat. The scheme wasn't in place yet but I wanted to understand how it worked. I was told it wouldn't be possible to buy my flat even when the policy came into effect. The property I lived in had been held on a long lease by the council. They had a few similar buildings in my street they'd acquired on this basis. They told me the lease was due to expire the following year and they planned to hand the property back because there were subsidence issues to deal with (which would necessitate a costly underpinning of the houses). I asked how this would affect me as a tenant. They told me I would have to move.

I knew there were substantial subsidence issues at the property. When I'd first viewed the flat, the cracks were so wide you could see daylight out of the side wall in the main front bedroom. They assured me they'd deal with them before I moved in. Their way of dealing with them was to fill them in and paint over them. Since I had been at the property, cracks were appearing in the places they'd filled. If it carried on the way it was doing, in another year I would be seeing daylight again.

James had not been happy about me moving to Frome – he thought it would spell the end of our relationship (which it no doubt would have). He wanted our relationship to become more serious and so asked me to marry him. I always swore I would never get married after experiencing my parents' disastrous marriage – plus seeing friends' marriages fall apart. So I was surprised to find myself saying 'yes'.

On hearing that I would probably have to move the following year anyway, we discussed the possibility of buying a house in his home town in Buckinghamshire. In the summer of '79 we decided to move forward with these plans because prices had continued to rise across the country. We soon wouldn't be able to afford to buy anything if we waited. I then asked Ronan for money from my deferred wages and he claimed he couldn't afford to give me anything. I wasn't even receiving my normal £10 as I wasn't working for him every week.

There was little to do on the film with no Dick or Tim to complete part two and I was only doing the odd thing here and there for him on behalf of Radio Caroline. He'd told me he'd set up some kind of new deal for Radio Caroline that he was entrenched in. He didn't give me the details and to be honest I didn't want to hear them, fearful that he was setting someone up to lose a considerable amount of money.

There was still money left in the film bank account from the £20,000 Ronan's business acquaintance had invested. Ronan would often raise the matter and suggest he could 'borrow' it for some other urgent matter. I always refused as I knew it would never be repaid. The balance I held was insufficient to complete part two of the film, but it could go some way towards it. A couple of friends said I should take the money for myself towards what I was owed but it didn't feel right to do that. As far as I was concerned it was to be used toward finishing the film.

Fortunately, I'd saved money from other earnings so had money towards the deposit of the house purchase in Bucks.

As it turned out, the council bought the freehold of the property in West Hampstead after I moved out and they completed the necessary works to stabilise it. I was told that the person who moved into the flat after me (who was a friend of a friend) bought the flat (with central heating added) at a very reduced rate a couple of years later.

Given that James and I never made it to the alter

and the house we bought was sold again within a short time frame, I gave myself a hard time over the decision I made. In the end I decided it wasn't worth hanging on to regrets and let it go.

With the collapse of the sale on the house in Frome, I'll never know whether Ronan would have kept his word and paid the agreed sum towards it. I'd like to think he would have. He claimed he had the money ready to send but as it fell through, it was spent on something else that became a priority.

The issue of money he owed me was never actually raised again.

21

James and I had kept in touch with a few of those still working on Radio Caroline. Conditions out on Mi Amigo didn't sound good from all we were hearing. After meeting up with Peter Chicago he enlightened me further.

> In 1979 the condition of the ship had deteriorated to such an extent that it had started regularly taking in water. In order to keep the ship safe, two petrol driven pumps were used to pump water from the bilges. The safety of the ship was dependent on these pumps working reliably. One day the crew on board were unable to get either of the pumps to work and the water level in the bottom of the ship became dangerously high. After unsuccessful attempts and hours passing with no results, the crew contacted the coastguard and a lifeboat was sent out to take the crew off the ship which was left abandoned.
>
> I was on shore at the time and as soon I heard via one of the rescued crew no time was lost before organising a boat to go out to the ship – otherwise it could have either

sunk at the anchorage or was vulnerable to pillaging from fishing boats or other vessels in the area. Or claimed as salvage. There seemed a very real possibility that the ship would be lost.

I went out there together with several of the DJs who had left the ship, under the impression that they we were all intending to stay on board and work together to fix the problem. It was an anxious journey going out to the ship as we couldn't be sure that we wouldn't find another boat alongside or people already onboard. When the ship came into sight, we were relieved to see no other ships close by. We could also see that the ship was listing heavily in what was a moderately rough sea. Because the sea was rough, the boat was unable to go alongside. There was a rubber dinghy which we used to travel across to the ship.

I clambered on board together with the skipper of the boat who had brought us out there and the two of us went straight down to the engine room to examine the pumps. Within a few minutes we had one of them working and it became clear that we could pump the bilges dry. We were only just in time because the water had already come over the top of the deck plates in the engine room. Within hours the ship would have sunk.

Once the pump was running the two of us went up to the deck and the skipper told me that he was returning to his boat. The DJs were still on the skipper's boat. I was waiting for them come across which they eventually did in the dinghy. Instead of climbing on board, they asked me to collect their belongings from the mess room where they had left them when they departed on the life boat. I was shocked to discover that they had no intention of coming back onto the ship but were simply there to collect their belongings.

I collected their bags but made no attempt to pass them down with any care to those in the dinghy below. Instead I hurled the bags into the bottom of the dinghy which was awash with sea water. Some of the bags burst open and belongings were scattered. I was asked if I was coming back – although it was obvious though that someone needed to be on board to keep things running, otherwise the boat could sink. With trepidation I watched as they boat headed back to shore and wondered what I had let myself in for.

I went inside the ship to the lower deck where the cabins were located and was appalled to see that the corridor was flooded with water surging back and forth with the movement of the ship. As the ship moved in the rough seas the water would slosh back and forth, creating a disconcerting amount of noise and vibration. It was quite a frightening experience.

The ship was completely without electrical power so the lower deck was in darkness. My first task was to prepare for the coming night. It was winter, the weather was very cold and the only heating was calor gas heating in the mess room. Internal lighting was provided by a tilly lamp. The external lighting consisted of a number of improvised oil lamps located around the sides of the ship. These were made from glass jars using jay cloths as wicks. They were then filled with diesel oil which had to be refilled every day. This was my first priority to ensure the ship was lit during the night. I then took a mattress and bedding from a cabin below decks and made up a bed on the wheelhouse floor. Because I was alone on the ship, I was concerned that the ship might sink and I had no wish to be trapped in a below deck cabin. There were life rafts attached to the wheelhouse and I made sure I had flares and life jackets ready to hand. I reasoned that being in the wheelhouse, it provided the greatest opportunity to escape should the ship sink. It was a very strange and lonely experience being out of the ship in such desperate conditions.

Once I completed these preparations I settled in for a long evening on the ship. There was plenty of food on board because there had been a tender just a few days earlier. I cooked myself a meal and huddled over the calor gas fire on that freezing cold night.

After a couple of hours, I checked the pump and saw that it had cleared the water from the bottom of the ship. I then had to turn the pump off.

For some time previously we had been aware that the ship was taking in a small amount of water. It was a concern but providing the levels of water were monitored and the bilges were pumped out at regular intervals it was not a serious problem. However, when the pumps failed it became a problem for those on board.

In due course I retired for the night to my wheelhouse bed. The following day a boat came out bringing two engineers and some DJs. With the extra assistance the situation was soon turned around and the emergency was over.

In the following weeks we investigated possible sources of the leaks and discovered there were various places where the whole plating had rusted through allowing water to enter the ship. On the advice of our experienced Irish Engineer, we set about creating concrete patches covering the affected areas. Despite all our valiant efforts to repair the ship the following year the anchor chain broke and the ship grounded on a sand bank where it ultimately sank.

James and I heard the news of the Mi Amigo sinking on the radio. It filled us with sadness. I felt quite down in the dumps for days following.

Despite all the hardships the DJs and crew encountered over the years and the shenanigans going on in the background, there were plenty of fun times.

James and others used to tell me about some of the pranks they played on each other but with the passage of time I can't recall them. Only one stands out – and that was that they used to catch baby 'sharks' (real ones) from over the side and lower them into the studio to startle the presenter who was currently 'on air' – making them yelp because there'd be some snapping teeth from the struggling creature. I recall this prank as I heard it a few times and it always made me shiver – I had a close encounter with a shark at a Sydney beach when I was a teenager and had to be rescued by a life saver. I've avoided swimming in the sea ever since – although I'm happy with pools and fresh water rivers. Coming face to face with a shark – no matter how small – would be one of my worst nightmares and I always felt sorry for the poor presenters who experienced this prank.

One of their fun activities was during extremely low

tides they were able to row across to the sandbanks and take some exercise – James told me how they once played a game of football on the sandbanks. Mi Amigo wasn't a big ship and the opportunities for exercise must have been limited. If they hadn't had the occasional food shortages, I'm sure they would have all returned home weighing substantially more than they did on embarkation.

The idea of Radio Caroline never being on the air again seemed impossible. I hoped Ronan was working towards a resurrection.

22

I obtained a full-time teaching job in Buckinghamshire commencing September 1979 and moved into the new house with James. He was working for United Biscuits radio station that broadcast into their factories around the country. The job didn't last and he filled the gap working with a friend who did removals while he decided what he wanted to do. Returning to Radio Caroline was not an option for him.

Anthony Summers wrote his book on John F Kennedy's assassination, releasing it in 1980 with the title: *Conspiracy – who killed JFK?* (I've discovered that he has since updated it and re-published it with a new title – *Not in Your Lifetime – The Assassination of JFK*). Tony approached Ronan to ask if he could have a few minutes of the interviews he completed to show on television when he was doing a promotion of his book. We prepared a leaflet about the film, which I believe was the first one we'd done (Ronan subsequently updated it and had someone produce a more sophisticated one). He had decided to call it *King Kennedy* by this time, rather than *The Kennedy Conspiracy* he'd previously landed on. I didn't particularly like the name *King Kennedy* – it suggested that John F. Kennedy was a King – but Ronan's argument was that it incorporated Martin Luther King's name. 'Only if you put an 'and' between the two names,' I argued.

Ronan expected Tony to mention the film at his book launch so was happy for him to have the footage he requested. He thought Tony's promotion would attract publicity for the film and possibly more backers. After discussing it, we agreed I would give Tony a licence to show the clips on two television appearances only.

I met up with Tony, he told me what segments of film he wanted and I arranged to have them cropped for him and assembled. I delivered them to his flat along with the contract. I stressed this was for *two* television broadcasts. He agreed.

I missed the first show Tony appeared on to talk about his book but I did catch the second one. He must have told the interviewer prior to going to air that a film was being made from his book. When the interviewer raised it, Tony agreed this was the case but made no mention of the name of the film. Whereas the truth was, he had written his book based on much of *our* research. I nearly choked on the cup of tea I was drinking at the time when I heard him say this. He also said he was going to be doing a book tour of the country and intimated he would be showing the clip again and again. This was not what we had agreed.

My phone rang immediately after with a very angry Ronan on the line.

'Did you see Summers?' he asked.

'Yes.'

'I want you to get that footage back,' he said. 'He's not to use it again.'

'Oh, I have every intention of retrieving it,' I told him. A plan had already been formulating in my mind.

I drove down to London, and sat in my car, staking out Tony's flat. It was on a weekend. If my memory serves me correctly, he lived with his sister at the time. I'd met her on a prior visit. After some time, Tony left the flat. I noted that he was empty handed. That meant he didn't have the film with him. I hoped it was in the flat. I left it for a good five minutes to ensure he wasn't returning for something he'd forgotten and approached the door.

When a young woman (who I think was his sister) answered I said, 'Hi, Tony forgot the film. I've come to collect it.'

'Oh, okay', she said. 'I think it's in his bedroom.' She waved her hand in the direction of his room and I walked in as calmly as I could and began the search. I found the can of film on the floor underneath his bed. I scooped it up and called out, 'found it, thanks,' on my way out.

I returned home and phoned Ronan. 'Got it,' I told him.

'Well done.'

'You know Tony will be on the phone to you badmouthing me when he learns what I've done.'

'I know. I'll calm him down.'

I could just imagine what Ronan might say – putting all the blame on me being some sort of tyrant with him acting all innocent in the matter.

'But you're not going to say he can have the footage back, are you?'

'Not on your life,' Ronan said.

'Good, because I wouldn't have agreed to it.'

I received a hostile phone call from Tony later that day. I reminded him that he had already shown the clip twice which was all he was entitled to do and that he didn't *own* the footage. We did. He was not a happy bunny.

I subsequently received a signed copy of *Conspiracy* sent to me by his publisher. Tony must have given him the list of those he wished to have a complimentary copy sent to long before our little 'bust up'. I'm sure if he'd remembered he would have cancelled my copy.

In his 'acknowledgements' pages, Tony gives just over two lines of mention to Dick Fontaine and Ronan O'Rahilly – referring to them as 'independent filmmakers' who gave him 'further research opportunities' – without elaboration. In his sources he lists some of the interviews he did in the US (which he was paid to do on our behalf) but doesn't acknowledge that they were done whilst filming for REF.

He also acknowledges his French film crew members

that cost us an arm and a leg.

Conspiracy was well written and I believe it sold well. It was a shame that we weren't able to finish the film and release it to coincide with his publication.

23

As the summer school holidays approached in 1980 Ronan asked me to look at hiring an editing suite in London and finding some editors to slot the interviews into part two of the film.

'You can decide where to insert them,' Ronan said. 'I trust your judgement,' – he added after I reminded him that I was not a director like Dick. 'We need to have a rough cut finished within the next couple of months as George is now available to put more money into the film.'

Month Python's *Life of Brian* had been released in 1979 and had been a box office success. George had recovered the millions he'd invested in it – and made some. I hadn't seen the film and had no interest in doing so. I didn't think I could be objective about it. A good friend of mine raves about it, saying it is the funniest film he has ever seen. When it was on television a few years ago I recorded it and forced myself to watch it. No comment.

Ronan wanted part two finished to a rough cut and

to hold a viewing; inviting George, Dennis, his business acquaintance who'd invested and, a bunch of other potential investors.

It was a big ask. I'd had a gruelling year with my first full time teaching job. I'd worked in ILEA schools the year before and they were so wealthy and well-resourced compared to Buckinghamshire. Buckinghamshire schools were geared towards the old grammar school system. Pupils didn't transfer into secondary school until 12+ much like the education system in Australia that I grew up with. Instead of infants and juniors, they had First (to 8+), Middle (to 12+) and Secondary – split into Grammar and Secondary Modern schools.

It was like stepping back in time to my school days when I went there. Chalk and talk approach to learning; old fashioned text books as the only resource. I spent much of my year creating or acquiring resources to make learning more interesting and accessible for the pupils – working late into the night. It proved exhausting and, after a couple of years of working with middle school kids in Bucks, teaching across a range of subjects, I thought, *never again*. Thereafter I only worked in Secondary schools – when I returned to teaching. However, I was to have quite a break from teaching first. When I moved back to London from Bucks a year later there was once again too many teachers and jobs were scarce so I started a knitwear business, with Brenda and another friend.

Back then what Ronan was asking meant I wouldn't enjoy any kind of holiday break. I didn't think it would be fair to Simon and I didn't think I was up to the task.

Ronan nagged me endlessly until I agreed. Simon spent much of the holidays playing with friends who looked after him during the day (and who had children he played with). He also went on a holiday with a family friend. I only saw him of an evening when he was home.

I found two editors through contacts. A Canadian woman called Joanne and a New Zealander called Jim.

Some days I drove down to London (if Simon was to be with Brenda and Claudia) but if he was spending the day with friends in Bucks, I commuted by train.

I collected the master film reels, the interview footage and other clips REF had purchased over the years (can't recall if the master and the interview footage was at Ronan's by this time – I think it was). I hired a suite that was equipped with a Steenbeck editing machine in the Tottenham Court Road area. We assembled all the interview footage and trawled through it to find the extracts I wanted. I had a carbon copy of all the interview transcripts I'd typed up and prior to hiring the suite had gone through them carefully making a list of those I wanted to use. I selected sequences I thought would fit well and we cut them out and put them to one side.

Joanne asked me to collect her from her flat in Wapping one day. I can't recall why I needed to. When I arrived, I realised her flat was in the warehouse I'd tried to buy back in 1972! The area still had not been fully developed yet, but was heading that way and was becoming a trendy place to live. By the early 1990s when another friend was living down there it had become a very expensive and salubrious area. When Joanne came out to join me in the car park that day, I asked her if I could inspect her flat, explaining why. The conversion they'd done was disappointing. The warehouse had been split into units with concrete blocks which they'd left exposed. I don't mind concrete walls (with or without texture), but I think concrete blocks in residential units can look cheap – as though the owner has run out of money. It also creates a dark atmosphere if there is no natural light coming in. I decided I would have done it a hundred times better. Another opportunity lost due to the short-sightedness of bank managers.

Joanne left to take up other work after a few weeks so it was down to Jim and me. The money I had in the bank quickly ran out. I paid for Jim out of my own money for a few sessions but I couldn't afford to keep doing this. Then it was down to just me. I had days left on the cutting room rental to finish the work. Jim had given me refresher lessons in the dice and splice technique using the Steenbeck. I carried on inserting footage and in addition to the interviews, I used other older clips I'd seen Tim trawl through at different times that I'd purchased over the years.

As well as the investigation into JFK's death, part two included revisiting the death of Martin Luther King and Bobby Kennedy. Dick had already put Martin Luther King's Vietnam speech into the film. I thought it would be ideal to cut from that to President Johnson saying how 'brave' the American soldiers fighting in Vietnam were and then use a clip of the 'brave' soldiers being backed up by B52s dropping bombs on Vietnamese villages – interspersing this with MLK's speech.

Dick had done a poignant interview with James Baldwin which I thought should be at the very end as I believed Dick had intended. The film was finally completed as best as I could make it with my limited skills to a rough cut!

24

Ronan congratulated me on the completion of the rough
cut after I delivered the can of film to him.

'I knew you could do it,' he said, slapping me a few
times on my back.

'You have to remember it is only a *rough cut*, Ronan.
I've selected the best of the interview clips to show our
investors what their money went into, plus added other
older footage – but my no means could it be argued that
it's a finished product.'

'I'm sure it will be fine,' he said – even though he
hadn't seen it. 'They'll be falling over themselves to put
money in so we can finish it.'

I thought it was great that Ronan seemed so
confident. He needed to remain upbeat if he was to
attract investors. But then he thought everyone should
hold the same passionate views as him about the loss of
the three icons; John, Bobby and Martin.

There was a time lapse between me handing Ronan
the completed film and the next viewing. I can't
remember if it was only a matter of weeks but I know I

was back at school by the time it was held. I think it was because Ronan needed to ensure all his players were available and could attend. He particularly wanted me there this time. We might have held it over my half term break.

I booked and paid for the screening at our usual Wardour Street viewing cinema (out of my own pocket). Quite a good crowd turned up but I only recognised a handful. George Harrison and Dennis O'Brien among the most important ones there.

Both parts of the film were shown in their entirety. There was short gap between the reels and some quiet murmuring – although I couldn't hear what they were saying. Part two started and the theatre descended into silence again.

There weren't the usual credits to roll at the end of the film. The lights in the theatre came on once it finished and then there was nothing. I'm sure a sound of a pin dropping could have been heard. My immediate thoughts were: *Oh no, no one liked it!* After what seemed an age – but I'm sure was only seconds, the audience burst into spontaneous applause.

Ronan had been sitting down the front over the aisle from me. I'd sat at the front alone. He now stood continuing to clap along with the audience, whilst looking at me and grinning from ear to ear. Well I knew *he* would like it. Now we needed to gauge the response of our main investor.

I stood and walked up the aisle, stopping at the row

where George and Dennis were sitting.

'Wow. That was powerful,' George said, standing and stepping out into the aisle smiling. The group who were with him followed. George seemed pleased. *Thank goodness.*

I could hear congratulations being showered onto Ronan behind me.

One of George's group stepped up towards me.

'Yeah, but it lacks the dramatic impact of films like *Apocalypse Now* and *The Deerhunter*,' Mr. Wise Guy said.

Both films he referred to had been released the year before and proved to be big box office hits.

In reply I said, 'Those films are dramatized *fiction*. They can't be compared to this film, which is a *documentary*, using *real* footage.'

Mr. Wise Guy was not going to let it go.

'Yeah, but it needs more action like those films if you're going to attract an audience to come and see it.'

I remained calm. I could see George frowning. I hoped he wasn't buying into this point of view. A minute ago, he'd thought the film 'powerful'.

'I'm sure there is more dramatic footage out there which covers the Vietnam War. But this film *isn't* about Vietnam. It is a *very* small part of the overall story. I think our film director, (I added this in to make it clear I wasn't the director) thought three *murders* would be dramatic enough.'

Ronan had walked up to join us by this time.

Mr. Wise Guy was like a dog with a bone though.

'I still think you need to get more *action* into your

film.'

George and the others started nodding.

'Yeah,' George said in a quiet voice, not sounding wholly convinced by the suggestion. Other friends with George, on the other hand embraced Mr. Wise Guy's views wholeheartedly repeating 'yeah' like a bunch of robots.

'*We*,' I stressed turning to point at Ronan (it wasn't *my* film – although they seemed to be acting as though it was), 'would need more *investment* if we were start searching for more dramatic or action footage, as you put it. The film, in its present shape, is only a rough cut. The point of this viewing was to show how we've incorporated into the film, the *exclusive* interview footage of witnesses we interviewed as part of our investigation into JFK's death.'

I said this looking at George and Dennis – had they forgotten that their investment funds were being used largely for that purpose? Today's viewing provided them with evidence that we'd completed the work.

I didn't add that our researchers had spent *years* finding suitable footage. It might have put potential investors off.

No one said anything in response to my statement about needing more investment or the original footage we had in the film.

Ronan clearly decided he'd fill the silence. 'Yeah, Lyn,' he said, jumping in to show agreement. 'You need to put more drama into the film, like they're saying.' A few minutes ago, he'd been smiling at me. Now he had a hostile look on his face.

I looked at him, disappointment etched on *my* face. A few choice judgements popped into my head about Ronan – and the other robots standing there.

I leaned over and in a quiet voice said to him, 'I tell you what, here's an idea. Why don't you hire a director, an editor and a bunch of researchers to do that then, because I'm none of those – or, do it yourself.'

I then turned and walked out of viewing cinema. I'd had enough.

I've no idea of what was said following my departure. No doubt Ronan heaped loads of blame onto my shoulders.

I felt very sad on the journey home. I had spent years of my life working on this film – as had others like Dick, Tim and David. Not to mention all the Radio Caroline revenue that had been poured into it. That viewing was a real opportunity for Ronan to pull in potential investors or persuade George and Dennis to put in more money. He could have expanded on what I was saying to George and his friends. Used his persuasive powers (and he had plenty of those) to turn their thinking around. Instead, he screwed things up by attacking me. I shouldn't have taken it personally but I did. I'd remained calm when communicating with George and his stupid friend – attempting to explain matters. But I reacted to Ronan. I began to wonder if Ronan ever really wanted to finish the film. I couldn't believe what he'd done.

As far as I know, George and Dennis made no further investment in the film. Ronan's idea that once he'd hooked them in with £50,000, they'd want to pour more into it, rather than risk losing their money, failed. With the millions they made on *The Life of Brian*, I guess £50,000 was small change for them. Hand Made films went on to make many more successful films.

25

Following the viewing I phoned Ronan and told him, 'I'm out. I'm resigning. I don't have the time or tolerance for your projects anymore.' I kept the conversation short and made no mention of my future plans or what was happening in my life. I believe he was aware that James and I were parting ways. I can't recall what he said in response except that he'd talk to me soon (when I would no doubt have come to my senses, was the implication). I didn't give him an opportunity to say much.

The sale of the house James and I had bought went through. I moved into temporary accommodation with no phone for a few months before settling into a longer-term rental flat. I made no attempt to call Ronan and give him my new phone number. We lost contact. I wasn't heartbroken about it by any stretch of the imagination.

It wasn't until the following year that I took action on removing my name from the REF company. I thought that in doing so I would be severing all connection with Ronan.

It was some years before I was to see him again. For

some reason Simon and I were passing Ronan's neck of the woods and Simon proposed we call in to see him. I didn't really want to but Simon had memories of Ronan being a 'great guy' and was keen to see him. On impulse I agreed and we pulled up into Paulton's Square and rang the bell. The curtains twitched and Ronan came rushing out to greet Simon as though he was a long-lost friend. Simon was a young adolescent at this point and Ronan hadn't seen him since he was a little boy. I was surprised he recognised him. He invited us in and, over tea, we chatted for a time, keeping the conversation low key. I asked in general terms how things were and he said, 'good.' I probed no further. He then asked how things were with us. I told him we were moving to West Wales, to a village near a town called Cardigan.

'I had planned on moving to Bristol,' I told him, 'but couldn't find what I wanted there so decided to move to Wales instead.' I refrained from giving the background to the story of how that came about.

'You're buying a house?' he asked.

I nodded. A look of panic crossed his face then. I'm sure he thought I was going to ask him for money. The thought hadn't crossed my mind. I'd long ago given up on the possibility of him paying any of my 'accumulated wages'.

Making excuses we left soon after. It was to be another fifteen years before I saw Ronan again.

Simon and I did stop at his place on another day a few years later when we were in London, but on that occasion he didn't answer. He may not have been home

– or he might have been hiding.

He did call me out the blue one day in Wales though – in the summer of 1989. I recall I was completing the first round of work on our second house in the area. We'd moved to a bigger house in a different village.

'Where did you get my number from?' I asked him.

'Directory Enquiries,' he told me. 'I remembered you said you were moving to Cardigan.' We weren't actually in Cardigan, but we were on a Cardigan exchange.

He told me Ernst had some documentation to send me so he needed my address. Otherwise he'd just called for a chat and to see how we both were. I filled him in on what Simon was doing and the business I'd started. Once he started talking about how he was I realised the real reason for his call. He asked me if I'd heard the latest news and what the British Government had done to Radio Caroline. I hadn't. I was so busy at the time, running my business and doing work on the house, that I barely ever watched television or listened to the radio that summer. Dutch authorities he told me, in collusion with the British Government, had boarded the Ross Revenge (his new ship he explained – I knew very little about the new Caroline set-up) which was in international waters and smashed equipment so that they couldn't broadcast. He told me some of the gory details. Ronan sounded quite choked up about the whole episode which had clearly caused him some distress and anger. I thought he was talking very candidly for someone who was paranoid about people listening in on his phone. Either he was calling me from a different phone or he didn't care if they were listening.

I was horrified to hear what had happened and extended my sympathies.

'We won't be giving up though,' he said. 'We'll be back on air in no time. And I'm going to take legal action against them.'

I found that hard to believe – Ronan didn't do anything official with his name on it as a rule. I thought he must have had a company with a third-party name on it who would lead the action.

'You should take action,' I told him. 'They shouldn't be allowed to get away with that. If you don't take action, they'll just repeat this kind of aggressive behaviour when you do come back on the air.'

'They're not going to get away with it,' Ronan vowed.

Years later I heard first-hand from Peter Chicago, who had been on the Ross Revenge at the time, all that happened. It sounded horrific. I noted that the attack was committed when Ronan's beloved Tory government was in power, proving they were no more his friends than the Labour Party he despised (really just Harold Wilson). He'd probably argue that Margaret Thatcher, the then Prime Minister, was not representative of the Conservative Party and that she was different breed altogether. I'd heard that argument before.

26

In the spring of 2000 Ronan called me out the blue again.
I happened to be down in Wales on my Easter break. I
had a different number to the one he'd used some years
before (the exchange had altered and BT demanded I
take on a new number). We'd moved to a different house
nearby and I'd taken the number with me. I wondered
how Ronan had obtained it because I was sure it was
ex-directory.

'Directory Enquiries,' he repeated. I made a mental
note to ensure it was changed to ex-directory.

'I need a favour from you. Your help,' he said. 'Do
you ever come to London?'

I was teaching in London at the time but hesitated
before telling him this. After folding my knitwear
business and selling the stall I co-owned at Covent
Garden we had moved into a smaller house in Wales
where Simon (now an adult) lived full time (the
previous house had been very large and incorporated
the business). I'd returned to teaching in London and I
popped down to Wales during my school holidays. In

2000 I had my own house in London.

Despite living in Wales I'd always had a retail outlet at Covent Garden weekend craft market for many years – which I paid friends to run on my weekend (I co-owned it). I'd come up on the occasional weekend and stay with Brenda to re-stock.

If you were English and wanted to move to West Wales, you needed to find, or create, your own employment. I was already doing the knitwear when I moved there and started a new company selling wholesale to retail outlets in the UK and exported to a number of countries. As the 90s approached it was becoming a tough field to work in though. I needed to move to industrial production or stop. I chose to stop and return to teaching.

But back to Ronan. 'What type of help do you need?' I asked him.

'I have someone interested in buying some of our footage (I noticed he said 'our'?). But I don't know how to find it. I know you catalogued everything. Do you still have that catalogue?'

'Yes. I do.' As it happened the log journal was up in the attic, along with various other film paraphernalia.

'Could you come to my place to help me find what I need?'

'Where are all the cans of film?' I asked him.

'In my spare bedroom.'

'All of them? All the footage from Elvaston Place?'

'Yes.'

Wow, that was a considerable amount of film. I thought there wouldn't be room for anything else in that room if all the film was there.

It didn't seem such a big deal. The tone in his voice sounded desperate. I decided it probably wouldn't take me long to sort what he needed.

'I'll be in London next week, but I'm not available until the weekend. I'll come over on Saturday morning. Say 10am? I could make it later if you prefer.'

'No, that's great. Thank you.' I didn't tell him that I was teaching in London full time.

When I arrived at Ronan's place, armed with a large carrier bag full of film folders, Ronan was ultra-pleasant and friendly towards me. He'd aged but then so had I. He introduced me to his partner Catherine, who was French. She was beautiful and seemed a lovely woman. Perhaps he'd settled into a long-term relationship and abandoned his philandering ways. I hoped so anyway.

Within minutes of me arriving he blurted out, 'You've just missed James (although he used his real name) on television.'

'Oh, why was he on television?' I asked.

'He features on the news. I've seen him reporting quite a few times.'

I nodded. I didn't really want to become distracted with a conversation about James.

'How's Radio Caroline doing these days?' I asked him.

'You can listen to it on Sky now,' he said and promptly turned the TV back on and located the radio channel.

'The ship is down at the docks in East London. For the time being anyway.'

'You have a licence to operate as a legal radio station?' I asked.

'Through Sky, yes. I have some religious backers,' he added.

'I don't subscribe to Sky, so I won't be able to listen to it,' I told him. Two years later when I did take out a subscription with Sky, I couldn't find Radio Caroline on it.

I'd heard about the religious broadcasts. I thought he'd sold out by allowing American right-wing religious groups on Caroline and he'd disappointed me by doing that. I guess he'd been desperate to keep Caroline on the air and these people always have money. Ronan had had religious backers before – although I'd never listened to them. These were people who thought homosexuality was 'sinful' and preached sermons against it. A number of the Dutch and English DJs were gay and I often wondered how they felt listening to this drivel.

He gave me a sheet with the details of what he wanted. I walked into his spare bedroom and was shocked by the sheer volume of film cans. I couldn't remember our film library at Elvaston being so large. He'd had fitted shelves built and the window blacked out. The task wasn't going to be as easy as I thought as the cans had been placed on the shelves in a haphazard way. My heart sank. I calculated that this task was going to take many days and I wasn't looking forward to it; being stuck in a dark, gloomy and airless space.

Of course, I had no expectation of being paid for this work. The word *favour* had featured in our initial phone conversation.

During our chats while I was working at his flat and in response to his questions, I told him I was a Head of Department in a secondary school in East London and so resided in London during term time. He asked me if it was well paid.

'Not bad,' I told him, hoping he wasn't planning to ask for a loan.

I'd spend a few hours at a time in the room and then take a break, grabbing some fresh air by the backyard door. Catherine made me many cups of tea (although I provided my own soya milk and honey). I also took a packed lunch each day as you could never rely on being offered food at Ronan's.

It took me four days, spread over two weekends to locate all the footage he wanted and to show him which cans held parts one and two of the film. I couldn't believe he hadn't been able to see them – the cans were clearly labelled. I wondered if his eyesight was failing him.

We had a final cup of tea and then when I stood to leave Ronan reached out and grabbed the carrier bag I was holding, demanding to know what was in it.

'It contains the same things it did when I arrived last weekend Ronan – things I've had in Wales for years.' I'd left the bag in his spare bedroom while I was travelling back and forth to his place. I'd taken the film log away though and copied the pages out of it so there was a spare for him. Perhaps he thought I was intending to leave my bag with all its contents with him.

'Oh no you don't,' he said. His manner and tone became quite aggressive which shocked me. 'You're not taking all these contracts and company papers. I know what you're your game is. You're thinking you can get money out of me.'

'What?'

It was almost laughable that he could believe I'd be thinking that. Even if he ever raised the funds to complete the film, one thing I knew for sure was that REF would never receive any money – if it still existed. Ronan had already created another company in the 90s and I am sure he would start yet another one (utilising the reels of film already in his possession). I was convinced he'd done it prior to the creation of REF as there were so many cans of film in the 'film library' at Elvaston. When I asked how they'd been purchased or contracted I was told, 'You don't need to know any of that'. A new company would make any previous contracts redundant in his world view. Including contracts made with REF, Handmade Films and the businessman who'd invested £20,000. Besides I was no longer registered with the company.

'I only have papers relating to Research Educational Films Ronan, and the company *was* my responsibility at the time.'

Chris Moore had resigned from the company (and I had dealt with it legally) a few years before I walked out. I'm sure Oonagh ducked out of it prior to Chris leaving. I can recall ordering new company letterheading paper from a small printing firm in Golder's Green with just Chris and my names on it. When I told Ronan that I was resigning I don't think he thought I would do anything about making it legal. He hadn't wanted me to add anyone else to the company after Chris pulled out. But I wasn't about to leave my name on a company and run the risk of Ronan running up debts I'd be liable for. I had passed the company's responsibility onto a guy called Bill R who I think may have come through our auditors, Jackson Feldman and Company – or possibly Oonagh – although Ronan had little or no contact with her at all by then. I passed much of the company's documentation on to Bill R. The bank account details, cheque book, the annual returns, the minutes of AGMs, the contract with the parent company in Lichtenstein. What I hadn't passed on was the film log and other bits. He was only interested in the financial and legal side of the company. Not the film itself. I had retained copies of the contracts. I discovered in 1983 however, that Mr. R had never had my name removed from Companies House. I had to take care of it myself.

'It's *my* company,' Ronan said. 'And anything relating to it is *mine*.'

He tipped the bag out, inspected everything in it, put paperwork aside and a few things back before returning it to me. The previous weekend he'd given me a new brochure he'd had made back in 1994. A new Company called Casablanca Productions had been formed to raise money for the film. When I asked him how it had gone, he just shook his head. I wasn't sure if that meant it hadn't raised any money or that he wasn't going to tell me. That brochure was one of the things he placed back in the carrier bag.

I was tempted to argue with him that day, but one look at Ronan's whole demeanour deterred me. His eyes held a wildness I'd never seen in him before. My initial thoughts were that his paranoia had increased. Later I wondered if he was in desperate need of money and was worried that I'd attempt to claim a stake in the footage he hoped to sell. What he planned to do wasn't legal anyway but I was sure he'd get away with it – or at least be paid a decent sum of money before the company/individual who parted with their cash found out there were issues.

He didn't thank me for the work I'd done for him over the past couple of weekends as I left – which saddened me. Come to think of it he never thanked me for the work I'd done for him over all those years. I believe he thought I had intentions of trying to 'rip him off' somehow. His hostility followed me out of the door – even though he put on a fake smile as I departed. I never saw him again.

27

There were always conflicting views about Ronan O'Rahilly. Some people idolised him and thought he was the greatest thing since sliced bread. They saw him as a visionary, a hero, a great entrepreneur or the man who successfully manipulated the election back in 1970. Others, chiefly those who lost money in his ventures, either detested him or were very wary of him. I didn't idolise him; I didn't detest him but I was occasionally wary of him and there were odd moments when I didn't like him, particularly when we had political or ethical clashes or when I became frustrated with his paranoid behaviour.

A particular prejudice he developed from his paranoia was about people who had suffered head injuries. One of our DJs was involved in a serious car accident where he sustained head injuries. When I mentioned to Ronan that he was on the mend and would hopefully be back with us in another month or so, Ronan said: 'No, no, he can't come back. People who suffer from head injuries like that are never right again. You need to sack him.'

'I'm not going to do that Ronan,' I told him.

'He might be dangerous. What if something were to go wrong with his head or brain while he's on the ship? We can't take the risk. Sack him.'

'Don't be ridiculous,' I said. 'His doctors wouldn't release him from hospital if he wasn't okay.'

'Injuries like that changes a person's whole personality.' I wondered if he was talking from personal experience about someone he knew.

'It can do. But you think Simon's great, don't you?'

'Yes, of course. What's Simon got to do with anything?'

'Well he suffered a fractured skull just before he was three years old. It impacted on his development briefly but it didn't alter his fundamental character. And believe me as his mother, who kept a close and worrying eye on him, I should know. He remained the same sweet child he always was.'

'Hmm.' I could see the cogs turning in his brain. Was he now going to develop a paranoid prejudice towards Simon?

'I still think …'

I cut him off before he could repeat his demand of sacking the young man.

'Let me be the judge of whether I think he'll be okay. I'm not going to sack one of our popular DJs because of your paranoia.'

I wasn't afraid of telling him he was overly paranoid at times. I had done since our earliest encounters – from the moment I first stepped into his flat in 1973. That first night when I entered his living room and approached the window (moving towards a chair rather than the couch in case he was planning to jump on me), he blurted out, 'Keep away from the windows. Don't look out of the curtains. Don't let anyone see you.'

I laughed at him, asking why he was so paranoid. I can't remember what he said. But later that night, after observing further behaviour, I told him I found him overly paranoid. Which was one reason why I didn't want to have a scene with him and why I avoided working for him more than a year. Thankfully his paranoia was not apparent in the majority of our interactions. I was always aware of its lurking presence though and occasionally it would rear its ugly head. I dread to think how bad it must have become for him as his dementia progressed. He must have found it terrifying. I would like to think that he reached a stage where it was obliterated and that he was able to live his last years in peaceful ignorance.

After some further to-ing and fro-ing, arguing our points about the recovering DJ, he finally conceded. The young man was kept on – and has remained a successful radio presenter across different stations to the present day.

At one point in the mid-70s Ronan was referred to by many as 'God'. I can't recall who started it. I know when Oonagh and I learned that our phones were being tapped she decided we should refer to Ronan as 'God' in our conversations and never use his name. I didn't think that word would fool our Home Office listeners for a minute. I cringed every time I heard her saying it and avoided saying it as much as I could. I don't know if she suggested 'God' because he'd already acquired the nickname or whether she was the instigator.

Ronan had many successes in the 1960s, all which brought him fame but not massive wealth.

Wealth eluded Ronan, which might have had something to do with the way he operated. He kept faith with the belief that it would fall into his lap with projects like the band, the King Kennedy film and Caroline Homes. He knew Radio Caroline in its 70s incarnation would not bring him great wealth. He was determined to keep it on the air though and perhaps some of his actions proved to be detrimental to the station.

The Dutch and British authorities seem have been obsessed with destroying Radio Caroline and any Dutch station who operated out of the Mi Amigo (and later the Ross Revenge). Imagine how much money the UK Government spent over the years attempting to do so. Captain Hargreaves (if Bob the mole was to be believed) and his team listening 24 hours a day. The home office had a whole department devoted to dealing with Radio Caroline. Yes, there were other pirates which popped up from time to time, but Bob the mole's job was solely based on Caroline. Then there's the boats Hargreaves hired disguised as 'fan' trips which ventured out to the ship in the hope of snapping a few photos of those working on board (although Bob the mole usually warned us when these were taking place so staff would be prepared – the super-efficient Captain Hargreaves conveniently planned them well in advance). It must have run into millions over the years. Imagine if that money had been handed over to Radio Caroline instead. The presenters and crew could have been paid a decent living wage. The ship could have received the maintenance it needed. Or a larger, better ship acquired. What a waste of the taxpayers' money that department was.

One could also argue that if Ronan focused solely on Radio Caroline and invested the revenue gained from that in the staff, the ship and the necessary equipment, the Mi Amigo may not have sunk and the station might have proved even more successful; thereby attracting greater investment.

Ronan had his fingers into too many pies. He spread himself too thinly. I raised this with him a few times. His answer was always that his many 'pies' made life more interesting. He claimed he was a typical Gemini, although he only just squeezed into this Zodiac sign. I too, am a Gemini, for my sins. Perhaps that why we got on so well much of the time.

At different times during our working relationship Ronan told me he considered me a trusted friend. I think there were *moments* when his sentiments were genuine. He *knew* he could trust me during the Radio Caroline and film years – the amounts of money I handled for him with never a penny going missing was testament to that. However, I was not under the illusion that Ronan and I were *friends* in the true sense of the word. We did have many enjoyable times together – with our games of backgammon and our friendly debates about John F Kennedy, Bobby Kennedy and Martin Luther King. He held JFK in high esteem – a man who could do no wrong.

Although I concurred with him on aspects of JFKs life, I argued against the deceitful side of his character – the way he cheated on his wife. Ronan of course, being a womaniser in a similar fashion, dismissed JFK's behaviour towards women as irrelevant.

For the most part though, Ronan and I had a friendly *working* relationship. Fundamentally he was my boss – although we had a peculiar arrangement and at times our roles reversed. Ronan collected people. I was part of his collection.

I was not aware of any other projects that Ronan instigated after parting company with him in 1980. In 2000 when we met up again briefly, he only made reference to Radio Caroline and selling REF footage. It wasn't until after his death that Peter Chicago mentioned the 'perfume project'. Neither of us know if Ronan made any money out of that. Unless Ronan had a private income (which he might have had from his father's estate) he must have raised funds by alternative means. Thinking back over all the years Radio Caroline income was absent, just how did he survive? But survive he did, remaining in his Chelsea flat (on a peppercorn rent I might add) – always with a telephone at hand. It was quite an achievement.

And although we didn't achieve the hoped-for outcomes (particularly with the film) and it wasn't always happy endings, working with him was quite an experience. I consider myself privileged to have worked with so many different people; Oonagh, those on the film and in particular the many who featured on Radio

Caroline: Mark Lawrence, Stuart Russell, James Ross, Mike Stevens, Roger Matthews, Tom Anderson, Tom Hardy, Stevie Gordon, Peter Chicago, Ellen (Samantha) – to name but a few.

It was great to hear many of the old gang again at the 70s reunion held on the Ross Revenge in July this year. Memories swept back seeming as though they happened yesterday. It beggar's belief that it was more than 40 years ago.

Sadly, not all the participants from my day are still with us. Radio Caroline remains though and Ronan O'Rahilly's dream lives on. Besides the presenters who have always brought us great music, this is thanks to those who are not heard, not seen, not known. Those who work behind the scenes. Over the decades there have been many of us.

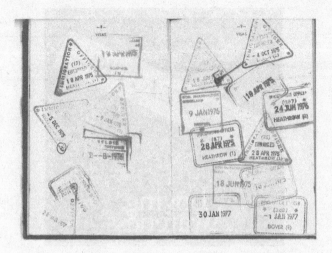

Two pages of stamps from my old passport
showing trips to the Netherlands and France.

**RESEARCH EDUCATIONAL SYSTEMS LTD
(Films Branch UK)**

DIRECTORS
C. Moore O. Leigh L. Gilbert

The first letterhead we had on the film company.

The band's album Ronan launched with the original 'Beatles' label.

The Band's single on More Love records

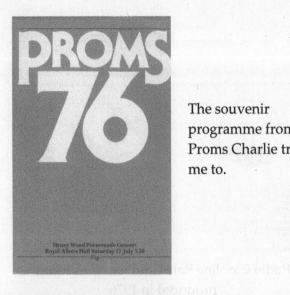

The souvenir programme from the Proms Charlie treated me to.

Author photo taken around December 1976

RATE CARD

Radio Caroline Rate Card for advertising produced in 1976

Independent research has shown that the
Radio Caroline audience in the U.K. alone
numbers 2.3 million listeners, not to mention
the European audience which our advertising
rates do not take into account.

More specifically, the listening audience
were shown to consist mainly of the younger
wage earning sector of the community, making
Radio Caroline a powerful, yet economical means
of reaching a most lucrative portion of the
consumer market.

For further information please write to:

S. D. Frances,
APTDS 14,
ROSAS,
(Gerona),
Spain.

Rates Effective From 1st September 1976 (U.S. Dollars)

Length of Commercial	Rate per Commercial	Package Rate of 112 spots spread over 4 weeks (4 per day)	Package Rate of 224 spots spread over 4 weeks (8 per day)
15 seconds	$25	$2800	$5600
30 seconds	$50	$5600	$11200
45 seconds	$75	$8400	$16800
60 seconds	$100	$11200	$22400

Other Packages by Quotation

Minimum Campaign period – 4 weeks
Advertising Campaigns must reach us 4 weeks in advance of Transmission
Rates include production and preparation of voice commercial if required

The cost of advertising in 1976 priced in US Dollars

Cover and spine of
Anthony Summers book
Conspiracy

More elaborate brochure
Ronan had produced
for the film under the
name of Casablanca
Productions in the 1990s.

Simon's Road Show Sweatshirt which he still just about squeezes into. A little worse for wear - in more recent years it's been relegated to being a top worn while painting and decorating. Note the odd paint splashes and the larger one on the sleeve.

* * *

Acknowledgements

Thanks to James Ross for being willing to let me use quotes from his old letters. Thanks to Peter Chicago for recounting some of his experiences. Thanks to Peter Moore from Radio Caroline – a fellow 'behind the scenes man' who keeps Radio Caroline alive today. Thanks to Jon Myer from Offshore Radio for sending me the wonderful photograph of the MV Mi Amigo at night and to Hans Knot, the custodian of Rob Olthof's library of photographs, for giving me permission to use it. Thanks to all those who have encouraged me to finally write these memoirs. It is my third attempt to write about my involvement with Caroline. Back in 1986 I started writing a comedy screenplay based on real events with added 'fictionalised' incidents. I envisioned Dawn French, Jennifer Saunders, Ade Edmondson, Rik Mayall, Nigel Planer from the Comic Strip Presents cast starring in it. I showed it to a friend who had had some success with his work being published. He threw it back at me and said: 'No-one would be interested in this ...' Disillusioned, I never finished it. Then in 2004/2005 during a year I spent in Australia, I wrote a 'novel' based on a 'fictional' pirate radio station – once again using many real events and basing it on Caroline. The night after I returned to London our house was burgled and my laptop and handbag stolen. My handbag contained my only back up copy on the first 'memory' stick I'd purchased (shaped a bit like a pen). I was only a first draft but I didn't think I could face starting it again. Then the film *The Boat that Rocked* came out in 2009 and I decided there was no point in creating a fictional story after that. Following Ronan's death in 2020 I was encouraged to write my own memoirs. I made some notes to trigger dates and memory of events but stopped at that point. I wasn't sure about using people's names. It wasn't until I had read other books about Caroline that I decided how I might go about it. This book is the result.

The following sites might be of interest to readers if they are not familiar with them.

www.radiocaroline.co.uk
www.offshoreradio.co.uk
www.hansknot.com
www.offshoreechos.com

APPENDIX
The Months of Horror in 1974

(i)

In order to understand how my life became so messy in 1974, I first have to step back to 1972. After moving into my flat at Oonagh's house in West Hampstead I decided I wanted to earn more money to save and buy my own place. I acquired a bar job at the 'Bird's Nest', a disco set up at the back of the Railway Public House in West Hampstead, that was owned by Watney's Brewery.

After working in the bar for some weeks my hands broke out in an itchy rash. At first, I didn't realise it was caused by anything in the bar.

As the week went on the rash cleared up. As soon as I completed another night in the bar, it broke out again. When this pattern repeated over several weeks, I approached Mr. C, the manager and told him I didn't think I could continue working there as I appeared to be allergic to something I was handling. I guessed it was probably the beer as it would constantly drip onto my hands from the pump.

Mr. C. asked me to accompany him to his office for a chat.

'I've been watching you,' he said. 'You seem to be honest and you're the only one not dipping your hands in the till.'

I was shocked by his statement and I couldn't believe the other bartenders were stealing money. I'd never seen anything like that happen. I told him as much.

'Oh, they're very good at it. You have to be quick to spot it. I can assure you they are. I know you're not though so I have a proposition for you. I'd like you to work on the door, taking the entrance money. If you're there I know I won't lose any money. I'll pay you a higher rate,' he added.

The idea sounded appealing. No more rash. More money. I wouldn't be on my feet all night (there was stool for the ticket issuer to sit on). It was an offer I couldn't refuse.

I knew the names of the doormen from serving them at the bar. They seemed a nice bunch but on my first night on the door I was shocked when they approached me with a handful of used tickets, asked me to sell them again and give them the money.

'I can't do that,' I told them. 'That's stealing.'

They laughed at my naivety. One of them remarked, 'We have a goody two shoes here, that's why C has put her on the door.'

One of them approached me again, repeating their request, acting like a tough guy. They played that part well. I refused but felt a little nervous. They weren't happy.

They huddled together deciding what to do and came up with a simple solution. They would re-sell the tickets themselves.

'Just keep your mouth shut,' one of them warned me. I nodded.

The following weekend Mr C called me to one side before I went on duty.

'I forgot to mention,' he started. 'The boys will ask you to re-sell tickets for them. I don't mind you re-selling enough for them to cover their drinks each night. I just don't want them to make a living out of it.'

'You're saying that I have your permission to re-sell enough tickets to cover their drinks?' I asked, shocked.

'Yes,' he said.

'Wouldn't it be easier just to give them free drinks?' I asked.

'No, because then my bar stock would be down. The brewery would have a fit. It's bad enough with all the thieving that goes on behind the bar. I also have to account for all the tickets sold. If a small number of them are re-sold they are none the wiser and everyone's happy.'

'Okay', I said, a little unsure whether this was some kind of trap.

When I told the doormen that Mr. C had given me permission to resell tickets to cover their drinks they were surprised and said they had no idea he was wise to them.

From that point on I re-sold tickets keeping aside the cash acquired which I passed to them when they went to buy a round (and they bought quite a few of them over the night). They seemed placated with this arrangement although they still re-sold more tickets in the latter part of the evening and shared money between them. It wasn't an excessive amount though.

I worked on that door in the remaining months of 1972 and throughout 1973 (apart from the odd weeks when I had a holiday break). There were a couple of alarming incidents. Tanked up heavily with alcohol, a couple of times the doormen went too far in attacking stroppy customers. Ambulances had to be called and I was really surprised that they got away with such serious assaults without charge.

One night the police turned up mob handed (I think with the bomb squad) saying a call had come in from the IRA warning that a bomb had been planted in the disco. It was early in the evening and we had to evacuate the premises while they did a thorough search. No bomb was found and so we were allowed to re-open.

Hours later they turned up again saying there had been a further call. The doormen had taken extra care to search customers that night on Mr. C's instructions. Just in case. Mr. C refused to evacuate this time. We all carried on – a little nervous. Why the Bird's Nest was used as a decoy was a mystery. For bombs did go off late that night in pubs on Finchley Road. One pub was called the North Star. No one died but it was all very strange. There'd been no warnings at the pubs where bombs were placed.

A small fire broke out in the Bird's Nest another night and the premises had to be closed.

It was early in 1974 when everything changed and I made a foolish decision. Watney's decided they wanted to move Mr. C to another Bird's Nest in West Kensington. The deputy manager at West Hampstead, Owen and his wife, were offered management of a bar and a 'Bird's Nest' in Paddington. A new Manager was taking over the West Hampstead Bird's Nest. They all wanted me to work for them – which was not possible. I told Mr C that West Kensington was too far for me to travel to. He offered me much more money to cover the extra expense of travel and babysitters. When I told him 'No' Mr. C was devastated.

I chose to work with Owen thinking it was the safest option. Paddington wasn't that far away. I would be working for a married couple. It would all be very straightforward.

The doormen split the three discos between them and recruited further men from amongst their colleagues at Smithfield. The majority of them were meat porters from Smithfield meat market.

Through them I had been running a side-line business for the past year. Every Thursday morning I'd trek down to Smithfield and buy meat in bulk. In the stock cupboard at work (at IPC Magazines where I worked) I chopped up sides of beef or lamb and split them according to the orders I'd received from colleagues and friends. I charged them very little above cost price but with the quantity I sold, it meant I had free meat each week. I didn't eat meat every day and as time went on, I ate less and less. I think handling all that flesh turned me off it. My friends and colleagues were happy as they had good quality meat at a very low price.

For some reason the transfer to the Paddington Branch didn't happen for a few weeks. Owen carried on at the West Hampstead branch until his move. Mr. C called me and asked me to go over to West Kensington. I took a night off and visited. As I entered the place, I noticed one of the doormen's girlfriends was selling the tickets. Her partner had worked at West Hampstead on a number of occasions but wasn't a regular. I hadn't taken to him.

The place was packed to the gunnels. In fact, I thought it was dangerously overcrowded.

Mr. C asked me how many people I thought were there. I can't recall the precise numbers now but let's say I thought there was about 1000. He agreed with me. He was only licenced for half of that he told me.

'Guess how many tickets they claim they've sold?'

I shrugged.

'Only a quarter of that number,' he said.

So, 250. I whistled. That was some serious money the doormen were making on the side.

'Now you see why I wanted you to work for me.'

He begged me to change my mind. I declined but told him he should find a different source for recruiting his doormen – not from Smithfield meat market – an agency or something and not let them put any of their girlfriends on the door. I don't know what happened as I never went there again.

(ii)

A group of us moved across to Paddington when Owen took over the premises. Some of the same doormen came with us plus there were a couple of new ones. One of the new ones was an Irishman called Pat. After working there for a short time Pat approached me and said, 'We're going to get married, then we can run a place like this ourselves.'

I laughed, thinking he was joking. He wasn't. He started following me home and although I never let him into my flat, he sat outside in his car for hours just watching the place. It gave me the creeps. I had another stalker. At work I asked him to stop doing it. It was as though he didn't hear me. He would often grab my hand and squeeze it very hard (so that it really hurt) murmuring in a low voice how things were going to be between us.

I became so worried about it I approached the manager Owen to voice my concerns. After thinking about it for a moment he suggested that we tell Pat that we had become an item – that we were a couple.

Owen had made the move to Paddington without his wife, announcing to us all that they had separated and were divorcing. So, it could have been feasible for us to become publicly involved. Neither of us had a partner. He said he would make a show of pouring affection on me when I arrived for work in front of everyone and let it slip about 'us'. If that didn't work, he'd have a quiet word with Pat.

Nothing worked. Pat wasn't deterred in the slightest. He continued to harass me and follow me home.

Several more weeks in Pat told me one night he thought it was about time we consummated our relationship.

'I'll be coming into your house tonight to make sure that happens,' he said.

The mother of an old school friend of mine from Australia was staying with me at the time – she was babysitting my son Simon that night. When I told Pat that Winnie was living with me, it didn't put him off.

'I'm sure we can find some privacy,' he said.

I couldn't find Owen at the end of that evening – he'd gone off to join some of his drinking buddies from another pub in Paddington. I set off for home, hoping to make it indoors before Pat turned up. But when I arrived, he was waiting outside in his car. As I pulled up, he climbed out – so I sped off. He jumped into his car and followed. We ended up in a car chase, driving backwards and forwards across Kilburn High Road. I was getting low on petrol and knew I couldn't keep it up all night. At one point when I thought I'd shaken him off, I pulled up beside Queen's Park, climbed over and crouched down into the footwell of the passenger side. It was cramped and uncomfortable but I was prepared to stay there all night if I had to.

After what seemed like an eternity, someone started knocking on the window. I screamed in terror thinking it was Pat. It wasn't. It was the police. They'd observed the car chase; seen our cars driving back and forth and they had begun to follow us. Pat must have clocked them and taken off. The police continued searching for my car, finally locating it at the park.

When I explained what had happened, they escorted me home and waited outside for a good hour to ensure Pat didn't return. I was disappointed that they weren't prepared to take any action against him.

Whilst visiting Sonny and Oonagh the following week, I mentioned my difficulty with Pat. Sonny said, 'leave it with me.'

From what I understood, Sonny knew some heavy characters. A few of them paid a visit to Pat and warned him off. He left me alone after that.

Owen, in the meantime, kept up his pretence of us being a 'couple' at work. One night he asked me if I would accompany him to visit a soul club in Tottenham. Having my visitor Winnie as a built-in babysitter, I agreed.

On the trip there Owen told me he had ambitions for changing things at the Bird's Nest. The majority of customers were white people. He wanted to introduce soul nights and attract a black audience. The club we visited was highly successful and after observing how they operated and talking to the manager, we left; Owen happy that he knew how to put his plan into action. On our way back Owen told me that he wanted to make our 'relationship' real, rather than pretence.

He had been kissing me at work in front of the doormen and I have to say I found myself responding. That's when I made another fatal mistake and became involved with him. I didn't view it as something that might be long term – I had plans for going to teacher training college by then; rather I thought it might be a pleasant interlude for both of us.

Our relationship started well – we became very close for a while. Owen put his plans for the Bird's Nest into action and it proved very successful. He opened the Bird's Nest five nights a week; two soul nights, a rock night and other nights a mixture of music. Young Black people started attending in their hundreds. We'd have a queue around the block on soul nights.

Owen asked me to move into the private accommodation with him at the pub. I couldn't for a time as I was still working for IPC Magazines but once I left there and agreed to work more hours for him, it seemed sensible to have a base there. Winnie had moved on by then. There were many empty bedrooms at the pub, so I decorated one for Simon and me and Owen furnished it to accommodate us. I told him that I wanted our own room and that I wasn't prepared to give up my flat.

I didn't stay at the pub every night – just a few nights a week. During the week I would rise early, feed and clothe Simon, drive across to West Hampstead and drop him at nursery. Then I'd call into my flat, let Buffy out into the garden, return to the pub, cook pots of food to serve in the bar and do a shift until closing at 3pm. Then I'd return to my flat in West Hampstead, feed Buffy and take her for a walk before collecting Simon.

Buffy was a dog that had been left with me by Hazel, my old schoolfriend from Australia (Winnie's daughter). She and her husband Jacques had stayed with me the year prior. Buffy (named after the singer Buffy St. Marie) was from the litter of a local dog that Hazel and Jacques had assisted in giving birth to her pups on my kitchen floor. They'd found the dog whining outside the kitchen door in distress. It was a few days before they located the owner of the dog and carried her and the pups around to her house (the owner lived in a property over the back from me). When they agreed to take Buffy, they thought they might stay in England but changed their minds, heading off to Canada – leaving Buffy behind.

I'd feed Simon back at the flat and might return to the pub for an evening shift at the Bird's Nest – or in the bar. If I was returning to work, Simon would come with me and I'd put him to bed later at the pub in our room and pop up and down checking on him while someone relieved me. Often, I took Buffy with me to the pub as she got on well with Owen's dog Ben.

The police in Paddington weren't happy with the increasing success of the Bird's Nest. Particularly on soul nights. Neither, apparently, were other businesses and residents in the area. Complaints poured in. That unpleasant aspect of life in Britain at the time reared its ugly head. Racism in extreme – which the population thought to be acceptable. The police started causing trouble, harassing people in the queues and made a number of arrests. Unjustified ones. They wanted Owen to stop the 'soul' nights.

They (the police) approached Watney's Brewery as they weren't getting anywhere with Owen. Executives from the Brewery visited a few times. Whilst they were happy with the money pouring in from the business Owen had generated, they were unhappy about the magnitude of complaints. After only a matter of months they made a decision to close the Bird's Nest and announced they would also be selling the whole premises. It closed virtually overnight. In the meantime, Owen was to stay on as Manager running the public bar in the pub until it was sold.

Owen was devastated; his dreams were in ruins. I'd noticed that he was a drinker, but after receiving the shattering news, his intake increased. He became bitter and an unpleasant side to him emerged. Our relationship was never serious but as he changed, I found it difficult to be around him. I handed in my resignation. We came to a mutual agreement that our 'fling' was over. He begged me to stay on, re-assuring me that we could just remain friends and work together until it closed. Against my better judgement I caved in and remained.

Prior to the closure of the Bird's Nest, a number of permanent and part-time staff worked on the premises. A few lived on site – a general handyman who took care of maintenance and dealing with all the beer on tap (I think his name was Gary) and a DJ called Dave.

Now we were whittled down to just me and the handyman on the staff. Dave continued to live there and another friend of Owen's called Steve, often crashed there.

Owen decided that he would make use of the empty Disco premises and make some money. He held regular 'parties' where party-goers had to pay for their drinks while Dave would play the music. It was invitation only – the public weren't admitted. Owen asked me to work the bar on these nights. What worried me was that he pocketed all the takings generated at the bar, sharing a little with Dave, and had no intention of replacing the alcohol or soft drink stock he'd used. I was concerned that the Brewery could charge him with theft – and possibly all those still working for Owen. Myself included. I cautioned Owen, saying he needed to replace the stock but he wasn't interested.

'Do it yourself if you're so worried,' he told me.

I did. Taking cash from the bar till after each party, I would purchase bottles of soft drinks, beer and cheaper bottles of spirits, filling the empty bottles and putting them back in the downstairs bar. Owen had his handyman clean up all signs of the parties in case someone from the brewery appeared without warning.

It was at one of these parties that I first met Brenda. She had been married to an Italian man who was a croupier and lived the high life in the Bahamas. When her marriage fell apart in 1972, she returned to London and was offered accommodation in Paddington with the brother (Chris) of one of her good friends (whom she'd met in the Bahamas). Brenda had a daughter, Claudia, who was four, going on five. Brenda and Chris were in a relationship when we met.

I was shocked to learn she was filling in time at the parties while Chris had another woman around at their flat. We became quite good friends and Brenda would regularly call in to see me at the bar, both during the day or if I was working of an evening. She also started having a fling with Steve – Owen's friend.

If there wasn't a party being held in the disco, Owen would invite large groups of people to the bar and after it shut and he might take them up to his private quarters. Sometimes he would offer them a meal from lunch time left-overs. What I didn't know he was doing (until I caught him red-handed), was sometimes if they were people he didn't particularly like, he thought it was hilarious to mix a large number of laxatives into the food (which was usually a casserole of some kind) or sleeping capsules. He had a regular supply of sleeping capsules from a private doctor he visited. We argued about it and I would have to throw out any remaining food left in the pot.

Also, around this time, he met a group of attractive New Zealand women. Stealing from shops was much easier in those days and they had decided to become professional shoplifters. Every day after their forays into the West End, they would return to the pub and spill their wares onto the floor for all to examine. I don't know what they did with these goods.

I always had clean clothes for Simon and I at the pub in our 'room.' When I went to collect them one day as I'd decided not to stay there anymore, all my clothes were gone. I always suspected that one of the New Zealand girls took them. It was denied of course, when I asked where my clothes were.

One day I discovered that Owen was claiming pay from Watney's for four members of staff. He'd left paperwork lying around in the kitchen. I was tidying it up when I spotted it. There was only me left by this time (the handyman Gary was gone) and Dave who was having his board and lodging paid for and was bunged the odd bit of money when there was a party. Dave wasn't on the list of those Owen claimed for. Apart from the handyman, I didn't know the names of the other two people, but against my name was a much larger sum than he paid me. I noticed that Owen's name wasn't on the pay run, which was curious. The pay details were for only one week's salary for those listed. It appeared that the money was paid each week into Owen's pub account. It had been some weeks since Owen had paid me, using the excuse that he was waiting for it to come from Watney's, but here was evidence that he was lying.

I challenged him about it and he told me that Watney's had not paid *him*, so he was borrowing my wages until they did. When I raised the matter of the other names on the pay notice, he told me it was none of my business.

I had an Australian babysitter at the time, Sue. Sue and her partner were both supply teachers but they took on extra paid work babysitting so that they could save more money for their travels. I'd stopped staying over in the pub in my room and instead had Sue looking after Simon at home if I worked of an evening. I'd apprised Sue of the situation at work and told her I planned to leave for good that Saturday. I'd had enough. I was also unwell and had been prescribed anti-biotics from my doctor for a chest infection. I shouldn't have been working at all.

I'd handed in my notice (again) to Owen; he'd accepted it and promised to pay me what I was owed on my last day which was a Saturday night. Near the close of my shift, he told me he didn't have all the money he owed me and I'd have to wait. He handed me an envelope of cash, which was a fraction of what I was owed. I stuffed it into my bag (which I always kept at the bar with me) but I was really angry. I told him if he didn't come up with my money within the next few days, I'd phone Watney's Brewery and tell them I hadn't been paid. I also said, 'I might also be tempted to tell them about the other non-existent staff you're claiming for.'

Unbeknown to me, my foolish threat sealed my fate.

Owen insisted on buying me a 'leaving' drink to share with the 'gang' (Steve and Dave were there) before I left.

They would all be sorry to see me go, he insisted. I knew he wouldn't be paying for it but it seemed churlish to refuse. He was being most charming and had not reacted to my threat – which I was regretting. He made me a Bacardi and lime, a drink I occasionally might have when socialising. I sipped my drink chatting to the others and then drained it in one gulp. I was keen to leave. That's the last memory I have before waking up, lying on my side, on the floor of my 'bedroom' upstairs, naked except for a navy-blue dressing-gown lying over me. The dressing-gown was one Bonny had made for me and I hadn't seen it for some time. I later worked out that I'd probably left it in Owen's bedroom months back. I couldn't fathom where I was at first and had no memory of what had happened. Beside me was a pile of vomit, and I had a very dry mouth so I suspected I'd been sick. It was lucky that I'd been lying on my side or I could have choked.

I struggled into the dressing-gown and staggered down to Owen's living room where I could hear voices and laughter. I recognised the laugh of one of the New Zealand girls. At that point I collapsed and blacked out.

When I came to again, I was back in my bedroom, lying on top of the bed this time. I could see it was daylight. My brain was still fuzzy but much clearer. The clothes I'd been wearing the night I was due to leave were lying on the floor near the bed. My handbag was next to them.

I threw the dressing-gown on and headed off to the bathroom for a wash. I could tell someone had had sex with me, but I had no memory of it at all.

After washing, I dressed and checked the money Owen had given me was still there. It was. I then went in search of Owen. He was all smiles and played his charming role. I asked him what had happened. He told me I'd stayed on for more drinks and then started behaving strangely. He claimed I had taken all my clothes off and invited all the men upstairs in his living room to have sex with me.

'You were on anti-biotics,' he reminded me. 'You should have known better.'

My immediate reaction was, *oh my god!*

I'd told Owen about a situation which had arisen when I lived with all the Aussie journalists shortly after coming to London. When I got up one morning no one was talking to me. Apparently after sharing a bottle of gin with one of the other girls the previous night, I'd taken all my clothes off and suggested we should have an orgy. Which they'd rejected of course. I was mortified to hear this news as I was a bit of a prude and would never take my clothes off in front of people. It was the first night I'd drunk gin for some years (and had stopped because I had memory black outs with it) and I was on anti-biotics at the time. We decided that the combination of gin and anti-biotics must have created the situation.

After my initial shock at Owen's statement, rational thought intervened.

'I only remember having one drink Owen and it wasn't gin.'

'Oh, you had plenty more,' he said.

222

'Who did I have sex with?' I asked.

'Everyone.'

'Who do you mean when you say "everyone"?'

'All the men who were present. Except me, of course. You know I wouldn't do that to you.'

'Who was there?'

'You don't need to know that, Lyn. Why don't you just go home. Don't give yourself a hard time. We've all done silly things when we've had too much to drink. I'll be in touch when Watney's send the money through.'

He put on a convincing and caring act. I left – once again mortified that this could have happened. I also felt so ashamed. How could I possibly do such a thing? Of course, that's not what happened at all. But I didn't know that.

Another thing that worried me was that I had come off 'the pill' only a matter of weeks prior. I figured that as I wasn't involved with anyone, I didn't need to take it anymore. I'd gained weight on the pill and was concerned that I was becoming too fat to fit into many of my clothes. It's laughable when I think back on it. I weighed a little over seven and a half stone when I stopped taking the pill. Now, as a result of my vanity, I had supposedly had unprotected sex with a number of men. I hoped there would be no repercussions.

I rushed off from the pub in Paddington because I thought it was Sunday morning, worried that Sue would have been out of her mind with worry that I hadn't returned home.

I was to discover that it wasn't Sunday. It was

223

Monday. I'd lost two almost two days. When I arrived home, Sue was there with Simon and understandably, was really upset with me. She didn't know where his nursery was and had lost a day's work as a result.

Not only that, but she'd been in a dilemma as to what to do. When I didn't return on the Saturday night, she'd visited the pub with her partner and Simon on the Sunday. Owen had told them I'd left on the Saturday night and he hadn't seen me since. He'd told her that he'd paid me in full and so I'd probably run off, abandoning my child.

We knew then that Owen hadn't been truthful about what happened. I told her about blacking out (but didn't mention the sex part).

Thankfully Sue thought Owen's suggestion that I'd taken off, was not something I'd do, so she'd stayed on at my place waiting to see what had happened. They'd phone a couple of hospitals to see if I'd been admitted. She was thinking of phoning the police when I turned up.

I offered to pay her for her loss of teaching wages but she wouldn't accept it. Not long after that incident, Sue and her partner left to continue their travel overseas before returning to Australia so I didn't see them again. This was in the first week of June and it would be some months before I was to learn the truth about what happened that Saturday night and my lost time.

I was thoroughly exhausted after finishing work at the pub but worried about money I took on some temp work. Throughout my time working with Owen I was still doing the odd voluntary day with secondary aged children for WHAC and continued with that.

Whilst visiting Oonagh one evening, she suggested that I join her for a break in France. She was heading off to Nice again that week, flying into to the south. We'd been there together in early 1973.

'I can't afford it,' I told her. 'Owen owes me a lot of money. I need to wait around for that.'

'Well Geoff is driving down to join us the following week.' We'd linked up with this Geoff in '73 and gone skiing together. 'You could meet with Geoff in Paris and drive down with him.'

It was a tempting thought. I could certainly do with the break. 'I'll think about it,' I said.

Before she flew out, I called around to tell Oonagh what I had decided.

'I'll come,' I told her.

'Ok, I'll phone Geoff to tell him.' She scribbled out his details and handed me a slip of paper with his full name, address and phone number on it. It's a shame I didn't look at it or memorise it. I stuck it straight into my handbag so I wouldn't lose it.

I met up with Brenda and told her of my plans. She must have passed the information on to Steve because the next thing I knew Owen and Dave were on my doorstep. I didn't invite them in.

'We hear you're going away,' Owen said. 'Could Dave and I stay here while you're gone. We have to leave the pub by next week.'

'Do you have my money?' I asked Owen.

'Not yet. Watney's haven't paid me. They reassure me it will come through after the closure next week.'

Very convenient. Owen was going to receive his money while I'd be away. I was due to leave in another five days.

While Owen moved away attending to his dog's needs, Dave confirmed that he'd heard Owen talking on the phone to Watney's. He claimed Owen wasn't lying about not receiving his pay.

'If you leave me your bank account details, I will pay the money in for you,' Owen said when he re-joined us. 'We'll stay here until you return – that way you'll be guaranteed to get your money.'

I wasn't sure if Owen could be trusted to pay my money into the bank. I knew he'd lied about my lost 'time' at the pub. I hadn't yet challenged him on it. On the other hand, if I turned him down, he was more likely to disappear with my money. I detected a veiled threat in his statement. *Let us stay and I will pay you. Otherwise* ...

'We would, of course, look after Buffy for you,' he added.

The question of who could look after Buffy had caused me some indecision about taking Oonagh up on her offer. I'd considered asking Vivien upstairs but I knew she wouldn't take Buffy for walks. She could have let her out in our large garden for a run though and would feed her. I hadn't asked her yet.

'Okay,' I decided on the spur of the moment.

They turned up the day I was due to leave with their bags and Owen's dog Ben, a basset hound. Simon was overjoyed to see Ben. He loved both Buffy and Ben.

We travelled at night by train, a late night (or rather early hours) ferry and another train into Gare de Nord, Paris. It was Friday 12th July 1974 (my passport was stamped as I boarded the ferry in Dover). Simon slept through much of the journey. I fell asleep on the final train leg into Paris. When I woke, my handbag was gone. Someone had lifted it while I was sleeping. I foolishly had a clutch bag with me, rather than one with a strap that I could have placed across my head and one shoulder. If so, I would have undoubtedly woken if someone tried to remove it. But the clutch bag was tucked under my right arm. All someone had to do was lean across and gently withdraw it.

It was morning when we pulled into Gare de Nord and I was completely at a loss as to what to do with the theft of my bag. I hadn't memorised Geoff's details and had no idea where he lived or how to make contact with him.

At the station I was told to report the theft to the police. Following instructions given I found the police station. It wasn't a pleasant experience and although they took down all my details, I'm not sure if they believed me. They spoke little English, pretended not to understand much of my school French and were quite hostile towards me. They told me to go to the Irish Embassy (because I had an Irish passport) and gave me directions. It was quite a trek. As well as carrying a suitcase (which was not on wheels) I had to carry Simon on and off. He could only walk so far before it became too much for him in the crowded Paris streets. He was just under 2 years and 9 months old.

I eventually found the Irish Embassy and was admitted to a crowded room where I had to wait many hours before being seen. A brittle French woman called me into her office and asked me to explain my problem. At least she spoke fluent English, but I wondered why they didn't have an Irish woman or man doing this job. After learning more, I suspect it was because the Ambassador might have thought an Irish person would be too lenient. This woman was hard-nosed. Many of the people sitting in the waiting room were there to ask for money and she claimed most of them were con artist liars who'd *sold* their passports. I assured her I hadn't done that. She was reluctant to give me any assistance at first.

'You're Australian. I've never come across an Australian having an Irish passport. How do I know you're not lying like many of the others who come here?'

'Don't you have a register of all people who hold Irish passports? If so, you will find my name on it.' I explained how I came to hold the passport.

She claimed they didn't have a register and I wasn't able to tell her my passport number. I'd never memorised it. I don't think I'd even looked at it.

With obvious reluctance she said I could give her *one* phone number and the name of a person to contact in the UK who could lodge some money for me at the Irish Embassy in London. They would also give me temporary papers. These was the only things they'd do for me. I gave my own phone number and told her to speak to someone called Owen. I explained he was my ex-boss and was temporarily staying in my flat while looking for somewhere else to live. Even if Owen didn't have the money from Watney's I knew he always carried a stash of cash on him. I asked for £20 which would have been more than enough for us to find somewhere to stay the night and return home the following day.

Simon and I sat there all afternoon waiting for the woman to call us in again. I'd packed some food for the journey but by this time it was long gone. We were both hungry.

Just before 5pm the woman called me into her office. 'I haven't been able to reach anyone,' she said 'and we're closing now.'

'But I have no money and nowhere to go,' I said.

'I can't do anything else for you,' she said shrugging indifferently.

'Couldn't you lend me some money so we can find accommodation?'

'No, I told you, we don't do that.'

'My son Simon is less than three years old. What do you expect me to do with him? I can't wander the streets.' The idea was horrifying.

She shook her head. 'That's not my problem,' she said. My god she was hard-nosed. I couldn't understand how she could be so cruel.

'When do you open again?'

'Monday.'

'You're not open tomorrow?'

She didn't answer me.

'You'll have to leave now. We're closing,' she reiterated and stood.

So shortly after 5pm on a Friday evening I was shoved onto the streets of Paris with a young child and no money.

I stumbled around the Paris streets in shock. Simon had napped at the Embassy and was full of life and chirpy. I worked hard to avoid showing him my fear and distress. Spotting a park bench I headed there and sat thinking.

For some time, I castigated myself with all the precautions I *should* have taken. Splitting my cash into my suitcase, my handbag or on my body – not putting it all in the one place. Back then you either carried cash or traveller's cheques when visiting foreign countries. I don't think bank cards existed then. I had collected Francs from my bank and had a couple of English notes that could be exchanged later if needed. I told myself off for not memorising Geoff's details. Perhaps the police might have allowed me to call him. Now it was far too late. I had no contact details for Oonagh down in Nice. Geoff would have given up waiting for me and be on his way there.

I was also annoyed with myself for giving my home phone number to the Embassy. But then I reasoned that it was the obvious thing to do. Sonny, who I know would have been willing to lodge money for me at the Irish Embassy, would have been at work. I didn't know who he worked for back then or have a number for him. Brenda, one of the few people who might have been home during the day had never given me her home phone number saying Chris didn't like people to call her. Everyone else I knew was at work with numbers I didn't know. It had to be someone in London so my cousin in Bath was out of the question. I could have called Ronan O'Rahilly if I'd known his number. I'm sure he would have helped me – however, he'd always called *me* and I'd never asked him for his number.

What was I going to do I asked myself over and over?

Back then I don't think people could contact a hotel and pay for a room over the phone. Except perhaps with something like American Express and I didn't know anyone who had those resources. So calling someone like Sonny or Owen, asking either of them to accept a reverse charge call later that night would be no help to me.

I then remembered that Oonagh and I had stayed a couple of nights in Paris with another friend of hers the previous year. I recalled the name of the suburb he lived in (I can't remember it now though) and knew his first name. Georges. Of course, Oonagh and I had driven there, but I thought I might be able to find it. It was the only option I could think of to seek help.

But how to make the journey without any money? I knew it was quite a distance outside Paris and it wouldn't be feasible for me to walk all the way there with Simon and a suitcase.

We headed towards the metro where I checked for the name of the suburb on a map. It turned out to be the last station on one of the other types of train (RER?). Miles out of Paris. We had to find a different station.

For some time, I observed people entering and exiting the station. It appeared that you needed a ticket to enter, but not to exit. Was there a way I could sneak in? They had turnstile barriers. There were attendants on duty near the barriers but most of the time they were engaged in conversation with each other, not taking much notice of the commuters. After hanging about for a while longer I came up with a plan.

I asked Simon to climb through the barrier and run down the tunnel which after a short run turned to the left. 'Mummy will call out to you but I want you to ignore me and keep running.' I then thought I could jump over the barriers calling out to him, pretending he had mischievously run in there by mistake.

'No mummy, I don't want to,' he said.

'We need to catch a train and I don't have the money for the tickets,' I told him. 'I'm really sorry Simon, it's the only way we can do it. Mummy will be right behind you. You will be safe.'

He wouldn't do it. Not then. But Simon liked his food and was hungry. I promised him if he did this HUGE favour for me, we'd have something to eat when we arrived at George's house. Eventually he agreed but with great reluctance. I felt terrible asking this of him and I was taking a risk.

My strategy worked. We managed to reach the platform without anyone intercepting me.

It was dark by the time we arrived at our destination. I then had to work out which way to go. Initially I set off in the wrong direction, but then retraced my steps and arrived at an intersection I recognised where Oonagh and I had nearly had an accident. We were driving through a green light and a car coming from the left raced through a red light, missing us by inches. We'd had a few near misses like this whilst driving through Paris. We'd arrived late at night and we were told that Parisian motorists ignored traffic lights after a certain time at night. We learned the next day they did the same in broad daylight.

I knew how to find my way from this intersection. It was still a distance to go though and Simon was tired. I carried him and the suitcase all the way.

Arriving at George's house we found it in darkness. It was too much for me. I collapsed on his front stairs and burst into tears. The neighbours (next door) were apparently packing to leave for their annual holiday and they heard me crying. The wife came around to speak to me. Fortunately, she spoke fairly fluent English. I explained what had happened and how Georges had been my last hope for help. Did she know where he might be?

He was away, the woman told me, but insisted I come into her house. They were such a kind family and immediately started preparing food for us once she learned we hadn't eaten for almost 12 hours. That's when they told me they were heading off to Champagne for their annual holiday where they had a holiday home.

'Why don't you come with us?' the woman suggested. 'You've missed your holiday in Nice, but you can have one with us instead.'

'That's very kind of you,' I said, 'but with my handbag being stolen I need to sort out a temporary passport and return to England.'

I also had to sort out acquiring some money but I didn't feel comfortable talking about this too much in case they offered me some which I wouldn't have been able to accept.

They were disappointed when I said no. The woman (whose name I can't remember) told me that her husband's father who lived with them, would be staying behind to run their business (a factory that operated from Monday to Friday) and Simon and I were welcome to stay on in the house with him until I could return to the Embassy. They didn't know when Georges would be home. They warned me that the 'grandfather' couldn't speak any English at all.

We were shown to a room with a couple of beds where Simon and I were to sleep. It was a guest room and the woman kindly made up the beds for us.

I thanked them profusely and then they set off on their journey, saying they preferred to drive through the night to avoid traffic. I can't recall whether they had children with them.

The next morning when I woke, I had a high fever. When I attempted to get out of bed my legs collapsed under me. The 'grandfather' was alarmed when he realised how sick I was and dosed me up with tablets of some sort. I couldn't eat – or drink anything except water. I also had a raging toothache which I was not sure whether it was connected to how I felt. I managed to convey to him with gestures and face pulling about my tooth.

The grandfather took Simon out with him for the day – I think they went fishing. The following day I was no better. Concerned, he called in a doctor. I can't remember much about it as I was pretty delirious with the fever. They spoke so fast I couldn't understand them anyway. I was prescribed something which I gathered were antibiotics (again) and took them without argument. I don't know how he managed to get the doctor to call that day or if he had to pay him. With free medical care on the NHS in the UK, it never occurred to me. It was also Bastille Day which, in my delirious state, passed me by until it was brought up after Georges returned.

On Monday I was still very unwell so the grandfather took Simon to the factory with him – although it was a public holiday. This pattern was repeated for several more days to follow while I was still bedridden. Our bedroom was near the kitchen and I could hear Simon and the grandfather chatting away to each other most days. When he came into our room Simon would tell me in a mixture of French and English about the lovely time they'd had. It seemed he was picking up the language.

The grandfather also washed and dried our dirty clothes, folding them neatly and placing them at the end of Simon's bed.

My eyes still well up with tears occasionally when I recall the kindness of those strangers.

My fever eventually subsided but I was left very weak. I've no idea what was wrong with me, except I knew I hadn't really recovered from the exhausted feeling I'd had when I left the pub. Perhaps it was brought on by stress. The medication seemed to fix my toothache so perhaps I had an infection there also.

On either Thursday or Friday, Georges returned home. After the Grandfather called on him to explain my presence and what had happened, he came into the house to see me and said I should move over to his place. I was able to walk by this time, but spotting my weakness, Georges insisted on carrying me. The grandfather gave Simon a big hug as he left us at Georges' front door, with tears in his eyes. He'd obviously become attached to Simon. They certainly seemed to get on very well, but then Simon was always a friendly little boy.

I think Georges managed to make contact with Oonagh through friends and let her know what had happened. I didn't get to speak to her though.

On Sunday night I told Georges I felt well enough to return to the Embassy the next day to sort out everything

I needed for my return to England. He offered to *give* me all the money I needed for my return trip but I was too proud and embarrassed to accept it. I thought he'd done more than enough. More fool me.

'I would be grateful if you could give me the fares for the train into Paris though and enough money to buy some lunch. We might have another long day there.'

He handed me a small sum of money without hesitation and wished us well when we set off.

(iv)

Over the weekend while with Georges, I'd thought long and hard about what phone number to give the Irish Embassy when I re-visited their offices on the Monday. Because I was going to insist that they attempt to make another call for me. They claimed they'd received no answer from my home phone number so I hadn't had my one phone call yet. I decided it wasn't worth them trying my home number again in case Owen had been out on a drinking spree and had stayed over someone else's house. I thought he might have become involved with one of the New Zealand girls. The only person I could think of was my old boss, Mr. Hill, at IPC Magazines. I knew the phone number and he was always in the office in the morning. He was often out with potential suppliers over an extended business lunch and might head off to play golf later in the afternoon. Mornings were pretty safe though.

Simon and I were one of the first in the queue that day at the Embassy. The same woman called me into her office. I explained what had happened to us and presented her with the prescribed tablets I'd been given as evidence.

'So, if I hadn't received such kindness from strangers, I might have ended up in hospital,' I pointed out. I was tempted to say a great deal more but held my tongue. I needed to her to do what I asked. She had a sheepish look on her face anyway, knowing what she'd done was wrong.

I placed a piece of paper in front of her with Mr. Hill's name and phone number, clarifying that he was my old boss at a company where I'd previously worked. 'I'd like you to phone this man. Explain to him what has happened and ask him if he would be willing to lodge £10 at the Embassy for me.'

I was only asking Mr. Hill for £10 which would cover our return fare and enable me to buy some food.

She opened her mouth as though to protest. I reminded her that I hadn't had my one phone call yet. Eventually she nodded and told us to return to the waiting area.

Later, she popped out briefly to tell me she had reached Mr. Hill, who was happy to send me the money. She was now waiting for it to come through.

Hours later she called me into the office again.

'I have your money,' she said.

'Thank goodness.'

'Here's your temporary papers that will enable you to re-enter the UK.'

She handed me a sealed envelope addressed to UK Customs. She also showed me a handwritten account she'd drawn up which showed the amount of money received minus two phone calls. I looked at the bottom line and realised that with the amount of money she was deducting, I would haven't enough money for our return trip.

'Hang on, you didn't say you were going to *charge* for the call. Otherwise I would have asked for more money. And why are you charging me for *two* calls. You said hadn't been able to reach anyone on the Friday when I was last here.'

'I did get through to the number you gave me. There was no one called Owen there and the person I spoke to claimed he had never heard of you. He told me I was probably dealing with a con woman.'

'What? Are you sure you called the right number?'

'Yes, I'm sure. So, you can see why I sent you away as I did. However, after speaking to Mr. Hill, who confirmed your home number to me, I now realise that the person I spoke to was lying. I think you have some matters to sort out there. It seems you have one good ex-boss and one not so good.'

I was furious. Furious with Owen for doing this to me. And furious with her for not telling me the truth – and for now charging me for *two* phone calls.

'Mm. It seems I certainly have a lot to sort out. In the

meantime, you have once again put me in a very difficult position. By failing to tell me what happened on that Friday and omitting to mention you would be charging me for the calls, I now don't have enough money for us to travel back to England from Paris.'

She shrugged.

'I needed *all* the money Mr. Hill lodged for me.'

'It is our policy to charge for the calls.'

'But you didn't *tell* me that. How is that right? And it looks to me as though you've given me a poor exchange rate.' (from pounds to francs)

'It's a standard exchange rate,' she said. 'Now I'm afraid I'm going to have to ask you leave. I have many more people to deal with.'

She stood making it clear I was being dismissed. I wanted to scream. I might now have some money in my pocket but it wasn't going to get us far. Another nightmare situation to deal with.

I decided there was no point in arguing any further with her. The woman was not going to give me back the money for the phone calls. If I encountered a similar woman today, I would be asking to speak to someone with higher authority but back then it didn't occur to me. I was too worried about what we were going to do.

I considered returning to Georges place. I knew he would be at work though and I had no idea when he might return home. It was mid-afternoon when we trudged off to Gare de Nord to find out how far the money would take us. I was right, I didn't have enough money for the ticket home, however the attendant at the ticket office assured me that if I could make it to the harbour I would have enough for a ticket from there. How to get there though?

I decided hitchhiking was the only way. I walked for several miles, carrying Simon much of the way, until I located the main highway heading North out of Paris and put my thumb out.

The first person who pulled up was a middle-aged man in a posh car. When I told him where we needed to go, he said he could take me only to the outskirts of Paris. I decided I would take a chance with him and it was a start.

The man was a headmaster of a secondary school and he warned me to be careful when he dropped us as the side of the road near his turn for home.

'I will,' I assured him.

Next, a lorry pulled up. It was dark green and had the look of a military vehicle. A man I judged to be in his thirties was driving and he had a young couple sitting next to him. There was just enough room for me to squeeze in with Simon on my lap. I thought with the young couple there I'd be safe and the man told me he was going all the way to the docks.

About ten miles up the road he stopped and the young couple climbed across us and got out. It turned out that they were also hitching a lift with him.

I wasn't sure if I should jump out as well and take my chances with someone else. However, it had started to drizzle with rain and we didn't have any protective clothes. I made the mistake of staying put.

Further up the highway he pulled off into what he called a Michelin Star truck stop.

'I need some food,' he said. 'I suggest you take the chance to eat also. The food here is very good.'

He went to sit with some other men in another part of the café. Simon and I sat near the entrance. I couldn't afford to buy much but with some money left over which Georges had given me I was able to buy Simon a snack and then we used the facilities.

My driver signalled for us to re-join him when he finished eating. We set off but not that long after he turned off the highway, wound his way around some narrow roads and pulled into large deserted looking clearing. It was pitch black by this time and we seemed to be in the middle of nowhere. I asked him why he'd pulled off the main road. He didn't answer me but picked up a radio and spoke rapid French into it. Alarm bells started to ring in my head. Something wasn't right.

He then stepped down out of the cabin, leaving the door open and lit a cigarette. Within a few minutes two further lorries pulled into the clearing. Now I knew I was in trouble.

Although the lorry I was in wasn't as large as articulated ones in England, there was a 'bed' compartment behind the front seats.

The two other drivers joined mine. One jumped up and ordered me to put my child down and climb over onto the bed.

Simon was sound asleep and I was holding him on my lap.

'No,' I said shaking my head.

He pulled a knife and held it out threateningly to me and once again ordered me to climb onto the bed.

I didn't know what to do. On the one hand I wished that Simon was awake and would start crying. A crying child might prove to be a deterrent. On the other hand, it might piss the knife guy off and he might do something stupid. I decided to take a chance. I'd never done anything to hurt Simon but, in that moment, I needed him to cry. I pinched him with my left hand (which the knife man couldn't see). Simon let out a short wail but then lapsed back into sleep. It wasn't enough. I pinched him again. This time he became more alert and cried. I felt terrible but I could see it was working.

One of the other drivers pulled Mr. Knifeman down and the three of them started arguing. They spoke too fast for me to understand everything they said, but from what I could make out, my driver had told them I'd be an easy target for some sex. The third driver who'd pulled Mr. Knifeman out seemed to have a conscious. He kept making reference to the bébé (baby) and pointing to Simon (who was awake and really crying by this time) and shouting at the other two. My driver kept shaking his head and pointing to the man's knife, telling him to put it away – which he eventually did.

I looked around and wondered if I should make a run for it. I had no idea where we were. I certainly wouldn't get far carrying Simon and taking my suitcase was out of the question. It was on the bed behind us.

The arguments continued for some time until Mr.

Knifeman stormed off and drove away. The driver with the conscience came and spoke to me in rapid French. I didn't understand him but the tone of his voice and his hand gestures were reassuring. He too, then left. My driver, who spoke quite good English, jumped back in and started to drive off. I asked him to drop me back on the highway. He insisted he would take me all the way to the docks.

'It's not far now and there will be no more trouble. I promise. I can't let you down on the highway at this time of night with a young child,' he said. But he could pull into a deserted spot and attempt to rape me. He had clearly set it up with his friends while at the café and confirmed his location on the radio or something. There was no apology. No explanation.

I didn't speak to him again. He kept his word and dropped me near the ferry terminal. By this time, I'd missed the last ferry of the day. We walked into the Ferry ticket office to find a number of other young people there in the same predicament as me. They were spread out trying to sleep on the benches. Before finding a spot for us, I took Simon outside (the rest rooms were locked up for the night) and managed to get him to empty his bladder. He hadn't worn nappies since the previous year and I didn't want him to have an accident. He then lay across my lap and slept through the remainder of the night. I managed to doze a little.

At Dover Customs I handed an officer the envelope the woman at the Irish Embassy had given me. He opened it and after reading it, snorted.

'What's this supposed to be?' he asked me.

'My temporary passport,' I said.

'This does *not* resemble a temporary passport,' he said.

'It's what the woman from the Irish Embassy in Paris gave me.' I explained how my handbag had been stolen on the train heading into Paris back on 12th July.

He passed it to me to read. I can't recall the exact wording but it went something along these lines:

The holder of this paper, (with my full name given) although Australian, claims to have an Irish passport which was stolen. We do not know whether this is true. We have ascertained that she lives in London.

Underneath was my name and date of birth and Simon's name and date of birth followed by my London address.

'You'll need to wait here while we look into this,' the official told me.

The Embassy woman had stitched me up again. Unbelievable. Several hours later they let us go and we were able to catch a train to London.

Six weeks after returning from France I received a call

to say my handbag was available to collect. I can't recall if this was from the local police or the Irish Embassy. Apparently, it had been found on the railway lines outside Paris where it had been thrown. Somehow it had made its way back to London. The handbag was the little worse for wear. It had sat exposed to the weather prior to being found. Apart from my cash – both French and English currency, nothing else was stolen. My passport was there; my watch and various items that disclosed my address. They simply, 'looked me up in the phone book,' I was told to find my phone number.

It was late afternoon by the time we approached my flat. I could hear loud music blasting out. I didn't have a key of course with my bag gone, but my upstairs neighbour Vivien did. I rang her bell and when she came down, I spoke quietly to her, asking her to fetch my key. I told her I'd explain later why I didn't have one. She was back with it within minutes.

I opened the door and entered an unrecognisable flat. It was such a mess. Stuff was strewn across every possible surface in the living/dining room – which also served as my bedroom. The double bed in one corner, the dining table and chairs, the spare bed that acted as a couch and the whole floor. The kitchen was disgusting. I don't think there was a clean plate or pan in there.

'GET OUT NOW,' I screamed at Owen and Dave (who'd emerged from the back room looking guilty as hell).

At that moment I didn't care about the money Owen owed me. I wanted them out of my flat.

Owen tried to play the inured party and look hurt. He attempted to reason with me but I kept repeating 'OUT'. He finally got the message and they grabbed a bag or two, shoved some clothes into them and departed with Ben.

I then spent the next few hours cleaning and clearing the flat, including stripping our beds and replacing the bedding. We slept with duvets by then – acquired during my time at IPC Magazines. I even swapped my duvet for a different one until my main one could be washed. While I did this, Simon played upstairs with Matthew, Vivien's son. I piled Dave and Owen's remaining belongings into the entrance hall. I didn't want them in my flat.

The tasks left me exhausted but it proved to be a cathartic exercise to exorcise Owen from the place.

The next day I went into town, withdrew some money from my bank and called on Mr. Hill at my old office to repay him. I knew he'd probably caught a cab to the embassy but he wouldn't let me pay back more than the £10 he'd lodged. In answer to his questions, I outlined some of my experiences in Paris. I didn't tell him about the hitchhiking or attempted rape incident. I let him think his money brought me home safely.

Owen and Dave collected the rest of their belongings from the entrance hall. They came when I wasn't in – Vivien admitted them. I had no contact with Owen during the following weeks. Needless to say, he hadn't paid any money into my bank. Either he or Dave, however, dropped an envelope of cash through the letter box at some point (without any direct contact). I heard a knock on the door and when I went out there, I found it lying on the floor. It wasn't the total sum of what he owed me but it was better than nothing.

Simon returned to nursery and I obtained some temporary office work again doing accounts.

Brenda turned up on my doorstep one day with Claudia asking if she could move in with me. Chris, upon discovering that she'd had a fling with Steve, had kicked her out. It was okay for Chris to have flings with various women, but it wasn't okay for Brenda to see anyone else. It was typical of attitudes at the time. So, we became a household of four. Brenda slept in the large back bedroom with the two children. We had to install another bed in there for Claudia.

A few weeks after my return from France I started to feel sick each morning. I recognised the signs. Morning sickness. That was all I bloody needed. A possible pregnancy where I didn't know who the father was. Before heading off for France I was vaguely aware of not having had a period. I couldn't remember when it was due. I expected it to come while I was away and travelled prepared. On the pill I'd had very little 'showing'. I thought my body was simply adjusting to the change. Idiot that I was. And of course, I had been ill. Not that it would have changed anything, but if I had taken more notice, I might have thought twice about going away.

A visit to the doctor confirmed I was pregnant. I

spun him a story that I'd had unprotected sex with an ex-boyfriend one night. When he asked me if I wanted the baby I said, 'No.' He made a referral to University College Hospital (UCH) for a termination.

After telling Brenda the devastating news of my pregnancy she passed the information on to her friend Steve who made a rapid appearance at the flat. It turned out that I hadn't lied to the doctor at all.

Steve told me what really happened on my last day at the pub. Apparently Owen had emptied several sleeping capsules into my drink. I'd only had the one drink. He then proceeded to tell me, as I began to feel the effects, what he'd done and that he planned to keep me at the pub and have continuous sex with me – as punishment for daring to threaten to make a call to Watney's. Me and my big mouth. According to Steve, I called him a 'bastard', grabbed a knife from behind the bar and went for Owen – but collapsed before I could reach him. I don't remember any of it.

Steve said Owen took me upstairs to his room, was in there with me for some time, then later dumped me in my 'bedroom'. When I staggered downstairs the next day and collapsed, he once again had sex with me in the living room in front of all those assembled there (the New Zealand girls plus Steve and Dave). He invited Steve and Dave to also have a turn, which they refused. Steve assured me that neither he nor Dave touched me, apart from carrying me back upstairs and placing me on the bed.

It was a believable story and one that didn't surprise

me. I knew Owen had emptied his sleeping capsules into pots of food a couple of times but it never occurred to me that he might do it with a drink. Owen of course, thought I was on the pill (as I had been when we'd had our 'affair' and no doubt thought it was safe to have sex with me). I wondered, however, if Steve was telling me all this to absolve himself of any responsibility in the pregnancy. When I challenged this theory, he denied it and reiterated that only Owen had sex with me. He said he'd try to find out where Dave was staying so I could confirm matters with him.

I made contact with one of the nicer New Zealand girls (I've forgotten her name – I think it was Julia) who had hung around the pub. She didn't really fit in with the others and we'd become quite friendly. We met up and I asked her if she'd been there on the night in question. She had been and confirmed the part about Owen having sex with me in front of everyone there and that it was only Owen.

'Did Dave and Steve carry me back upstairs?' I asked her.

'Yes, and they came straight back down,' she confirmed. Meaning they wouldn't have had time to rape me.

I also met up with Dave and he told me the same story as Steve. I believed them. Owen was turning out to be a prize bastard. He had borrowed heavily from a number of landlords around Paddington and other 'friends' he'd made in the area and, although he had since been paid by Watney's, he'd made no attempt to repay anyone.

Apparently, he was crashing at the flat one of the New Zealand girls and had applied to emigrate to NZ. Dave said he'd passed on the news about my pregnancy to Owen, who'd said he'd call me. I wasn't holding my breath waiting for that call.

I received an appointment to attend UCH to discuss the 'termination'. I had no idea what to expect but was horrified to discover how it worked. I was shown into what turned out to be a lecturing theatre. UCH, I was told, was a teaching hospital. A gynaecologist gave me an internal examination in front of many students then invited them all to do the same. It was so humiliating. I felt as though I was being sexually assaulted by a multitude of men – and they were all men; there were no women. I was then told there would be a second stage in the process where my 'case' would be discussed and a decision made. The second stage turned out to be a panel I faced – again with many student doctors watching on. I said little except to confirm the information they read out to me. I was discussed as though I wasn't in the room. It became too much for me and I stood and walked out.

They approved the termination in my absence and sent me a letter confirming a date I was due to go into the hospital. I couldn't do it. The whole thing made me feel so sick. I made an appointment with my doctor where I told him that I couldn't go through with the termination.

'You've decided to have the baby?' he asked.

'No,' I said. 'I'm not having this baby. I refuse to.'

'You're not going to do something stupid, like sticking knitting needles up inside yourself are you?' he asked.

I grimaced. 'No, of course not, I just refuse to have a child where I played no conscious part in its conception.'

He looked at me with a puzzled expression. I almost told him then what had really happened but kept quiet.

'I won't cancel the appointment, in case you change your mind,' he said as I stood to leave.

To this day I have always believed that I brought on the miscarriage – with a little help from Owen. Owen made his final call to me a few nights later. 'How could you be pregnant?' he asked. 'I thought you were on the pill?' I told him I'd come off it. Initially he stuck to the lie he'd told me.

I told him that Dave, Steve and 'Julia' had told me the truth.

'Ah,' he said. 'Well you need to get rid of it. I don't want anything to do with it and I won't be around anyway.' He confirmed that he planned to move to New Zealand.

'You raped me Owen, while I was unconscious – more than once apparently.'

'You were asking for it,' he claimed 'and loved every minute of it.'

'How could I love every minute of it when I was unconscious and not a participant? And what do you mean I was asking for it? Do you mean as a punishment?'

He said nothing further and terminated the call

before I had the opportunity to challenge him about what he'd told the woman at the Irish Embassy.

I worked myself up into a rage. I wanted to smash the place up – but being a practical person (who couldn't afford to destroy her belongings) I chose beat up one of my pillows instead – as though it was Owen. Feathers flew everywhere. I called it every name under the sun. When my rage dissipated, I lay with my hands on my stomach, talking out loud to the embryo, explaining that I didn't want it and why. I told it, it had to leave my body. The next morning, after cleaning the mess around my bed, I started bleeding.

I was admitted to UCH. A lovely female Indian doctor approached me saying she thought it might be possible for me to carry the baby to full term – but it would necessitate me spending a lot of time in bed.

'No, No, I'm miscarrying,' I told her. She gave me a puzzled expression and moved away.

Next a Chinese Australian doctor approached me. 'I noticed you were booked in for a termination that you didn't attend,' he started. 'So, we may as well whip you down and terminate it now.'

'No thank you,' I said. 'I'm miscarrying.'

He became angry with me and stormed off.

A couple of days later, after the pains came thick and fast, I miscarried. I was taken down for a D & C where I encountered the Australian doctor again. 'All that stupid fuss about miscarrying was totally unnecessary,' he said in a hostile angry tone. My heartbeat increased in fear as I faded under the anaesthetic.

The following day the lovely female doctor approached me again. 'I'm so sorry that you lost your little girl,' she said. *Little girl?* I don't know how on earth she was able to determine the gender. I was only a little over three months gone by the time I miscarried. I could have done without knowing a gender.

When I was expecting Simon, my stomach remained abnormally flat until I was about five months pregnant. With this one though, there'd been a rapid growth. By the time I miscarried, I was enormous. I looked, as a woman in a normal pregnancy might, a good four or five months pregnant. It must have been a huge foetus. The miscarriage was certainly painful.

I'm sure I looked confused after the doctor made this statement. 'No one told you it was a little girl?' she asked me.

I shook my head, unable to speak. 'I'm so sorry,' she repeated. I've often wondered if she mixed me up with another patient.

It was another four days before I was discharged from hospital and returned home.

(vi)

Brenda had been taking Simon to nursery while I was in hospital. On the first morning after I returned home, I decided I would walk him to nursery myself – perhaps a little later than I would normally do if I was going to work. I'd had so little exercise for what seemed like weeks. Assuring Brenda I was fine, she set off with Claudia, taking her to school.

When Simon was ready, we exited the front door. The house we were living in was starting to fall apart. Camden Council had earmarked it and a number of similar other houses in the street for demolition. They intended to build a terrace of townhouses so saw no need for maintaining the buildings which were let on a short-life licence to the Housing Association. Every time it rained, little bits of rubble from the overhanging porch dropped onto the landing immediately outside the door. The houses were huge and the drop down into the basement well on the right-hand side was considerable. The left-hand side dropped a few feet to ground level so it wasn't as dangerous. Normally there would be chicken wire strung across the right-hand for safety as well as a plastic crate the milkman left permanently in situ.

However, the wire had been ripped out shortly before I went into hospital by male dogs attempting to gain entrance to the flat to reach Buffy who had been in heat. After ripping out the wire, they leapt across to the bay window trying to get in. I caught a couple attempting to crawl in the open window so we had to keep it closed unless we sat there on lookout duty. Brenda and I had never seen anything like it. We were deluged day and night by these howling male dogs, all desperate to reach Buffy; both at the back and front of the house. In the middle of one night the French doors that led off the kitchen into the garden burst open and when Brenda and I rushed out there we were confronted with a mass of bodies tumbling around. We beat most of the dogs off to discover poor Buffy underneath them stuck with a black labrador. We were to learn that the Labrador impregnated her. Presumably her scent then vanished as the male dogs disappeared overnight.

The milkman had removed the milk crate that normally sat on the edge as Vivien was away and he didn't see the need to leave the crate for just one household.

That morning, Simon charged out of the door and as I was calling out 'wait', he tripped over a bit of rubble and somersaulted over the right-hand edge of the stairs into the basement well. If the wire and milk crate had been there, he would have tumbled back onto the porch. I saw it all happening in slow motion. I reach out in an attempt to grab him but I was too far away.

The base of the well was concrete, but fortunately it was full of mushy leaves that had built up over the years and never been cleared. The only way to access the area was to jump down there from the front garden or to climb out of the window of front room in the basement flat. The access to the basement flat was around the side of the building.

The leaves softened Simon's fall – otherwise he would have been killed outright.

I screamed and called out to people over the road (several were outside their front doors that morning) or those passing, asking them to call an ambulance as my little boy had had a serious fall. They all stood staring at me dumfounded. Perhaps some of them had even witnessed his fall. I repeated my request and, after running down the stairs to the front, I jumped down into the well. Even standing it was several feet above my head to the ground level and there was no way I would be able to climb out of there again unaided. Simon was unconscious and not moving. I wanted to lift him up out of the filth that was underneath him, but I didn't dare move him.

It seemed like an eternity before the ambulance arrived. They moved Simon onto a stretcher and lifted him out before helping me up. We were taken to the old Royal Free hospital in Hampstead. Simon disappeared behind closed doors and I wasn't allowed to be with him.

Sometime later a doctor came to see me saying Simon had suffered a posterior fracture to his skull, but there no reason to believe he wouldn't make a full recovery. He told me he was still in a coma, but breathing independently and was going to be moved to a children's ward.

The ward was located in an old building, several floors up and I was to learn the section Simon was in was for very serious cases. That seemed ominous.

Brenda joined me with Claudia after she collected her from school. I'd phoned my flat from a public phone at the hospital to tell her what had happened while waiting to hear from the doctors. Simon stirred briefly yelling out, 'Buffy, Ben'. He must have been dreaming of them. It made us burst into tears and gave us hope for him regaining consciousness. He remained unconscious at that point though. Brenda and Claudia were later asked to leave. I was allowed to stay on but at 11pm they told me I, also, had to leave. They wouldn't let me stay overnight with him, claiming they didn't have the facilities to accommodate me. I told them I was happy to sit there all night but they refused.

I caught a cab home but couldn't sleep so phoned my parents in Australia to give them the news. I returned to the hospital first thing the following morning to find Simon still unconscious. According to the nurses, he'd stirred a couple of times, but had not fully woken.

'This is normal and nothing to worry about,' they said, attempting to reassure me. I wasn't reassured.

There were about five other young children in Simon's section, most of them toddlers in cots. I rarely saw any members of their families and a couple had no visitors throughout the time I was there. For much of the day the children were awake and crying. Nurses seemed sparse so several times I moved around chatting to them, attempting to bring them some sort of comfort. I wasn't told what was wrong with them (confidential information I supposed) or why a couple of them never had visitors. It seemed so sad.

It was days before Simon was awake and fully alert. He didn't speak though and that worried me because he was a prolific chatterbox. Did he have brain damage? I asked the doctor. He insisted Simon wouldn't suffer any ill effects to his brain from the fracture and his loss of speech was simply due to the trauma his body had suffered. How could he be so sure, I wondered.

Simon's motor skills were also affected I noticed when he regained consciousness. He had been feeding himself for several years, but now he seemed incapable of doing so or even holding a cup. I knew this could happen as I'd suffered a similar impact on my motor skills after being in a coma following an accident when I was 19. I was aware of it though and worked hard to overcome my problems. I wondered if Simon could do the same. When I discussed it with the doctor, he suggested we stop feeding him to force him to respond. I was sceptical but agreed to give it a go.

Seated in a high chair, a bowl of ice cream was placed before Simon and we stepped back. His eyes lit up at the sight of it but he turned to me, expecting me to feed it to him. Brenda was with me that day and we encouraged Simon to pick up the spoon and feed himself. The doctor and a nurse stood by observing.

Simon shook his head – so he understood us.

'Come on Simon,' we urged.

Eventually he grabbed the spoon, not holding it as securely as he normally would have. After dipping the spoon into the ice cream, he scooped it up and raised it. His hand shook and he seemed unable to control the movements. It all dribbled down his front. His face took on a dejected look that he'd made since he was a baby. I instinctively went to move to him, but the doctor grabbed my arm and shook his head.

'Come on Simon, you're doing well,' I said. 'Have another go.'

He tried again – this time the ice cream ended up on the floor but he'd made movements towards his mouth.

'And again,' I urged.

The next time the spoon wavered around in front of his face for several seconds before he was able to land it in his mouth. He gave a big satisfied smile. We all applauded him. There was no holding him back after that. The doctor's strategy had worked.

The hospital gave Simon an x-ray before releasing him.

'All's healing well,' they told me. 'Just make sure he takes it easy for a bit. No vigorous running around for a while.'

I had to take him back for a final x-ray the following month and another visit six months later where they discharged Simon saying there were no concerning issues and he had made a full recovery.

After some weeks of almost silent communications, Simon lapsed back into his chatty self. Being around Claudia helped him in this vein as she was also a chatty child. Simon started wetting the bed some nights though – something he'd been free of since he was about 18 months old.

One day while we were out Owen turned up to drop Ben off (I was sure he must have been watching the place and waited until we left the house). Vivien allowed him to leave the dog thinking it had all been arranged. He'd enclosed a note saying that as he was heading off to New

Zealand, it wasn't practical for him to keep Ben. It was yet another imposition he'd dumped on me. Much as I liked Ben, (although he had a stubborn character and bad habits Owen had allowed him to develop through neglect) I didn't want another dog. Of course, Simon was over the moon that Ben had joined our household. I warned him I would be finding a home for him as soon as I could.

(vii)

It was mid-September when Simon came out of hospital. I was due to start teacher training college in another week. Even though I was determined, I had begun to think I wasn't going to make it with everything that had been happening.

Brenda encouraged me to start on my due date saying as Simon needed to remain off nursery for another week or two, she'd look after him. She thought that after all I'd been through and the effort I'd made to gain my college place, I couldn't let it slip away. I knew he'd be safe in her hands.

I'd received a letter saying I had to go into the college to sign for my grant and this was due to happen the day after my conversation with Brenda. I drove down to Wimbledon and joined a long queue. Before I made it to the front desk I started haemorrhaging. I was wearing

261

trousers and it embarrassingly ran through everything. I rushed back to my car, dragged an old rug from the boot and placed it on the seat. This was the second time this had happened to me since my discharge from hospital. Fortunately, the first time it happened I was at home and it was late at night. The excessive bleeding stopped after about ten minutes, leaving me feeling faint and I wasn't sure what to do. Before going to see Simon in hospital the next day, I visited my doctor explaining what had happened and that I'd been experiencing pains much like labour pains. He had another young man in the surgery with him and I assumed it was a trainee doctor. He didn't examine me and sent me on my way assuring me it was post miscarriage normal bleeding.

Now here it had happened again. I waited until the feeling of dizziness passed and drove home. After washing and changing into clean clothes, I drove to the surgery asking for an emergency appointment with my doctor. I was sure what was happening to me was not normal.

The doctor erupted when I told him what happened. 'I'm sick of you women coming in here with your imaginary complaints. I'm not going to examine you,' he shouted at me.

'I can assure you I'm not imagining it,' I told him. 'If you like, I can go home and return with my soiled clothes.' I hadn't yet put them into a bowl to soak.

He walked out of the room and apparently out of the surgery. I went to the reception desk to lodge a complaint.

'Doctor M has been under a lot of strain,' I was told. Many young housewives had been going to see him claiming they had gynaecological issues she told me in a quiet voice – when really, they had nothing wrong with them. Doctor M. was a good-looking young man and several patients had fallen in love with him. The other young man who had been with him in the surgery was there as a witness for Doctor M. to stop the women behaving inappropriately with him. She told me Doctor M was leaving that day and they had a new *female* doctor starting the next day. I made an appointment to see her.

Doctor L, the new female doctor, immediately carried out an internal examination when I told her what had been happening. It turned out that I had a womb infection. When I asked her if it could have happened because the hospital hadn't cleaned me out properly in the D & C, she said 'maybe'. She wasn't prepared to give me a categorical 'yes'. I was suspicious that the Australian doctor had deliberately given me shabby care. Either that or he was just too angry with me to be bothered to do the job properly. Sadly, his attitude was typical of what women were put through in the 1970s.

With the medication I was prescribed, I was soon well enough to start college and move on to a new chapter in my life. A new chapter that would lead to me working for Ronan O'Rahilly and Radio Caroline.

CPSIA information can be obtained
at www.ICGtesting.com
Printed in the USA
LVHW092117250323
742623LV00011B/116